Successful
PRACTICE SALES

The Complete Guide to
Buying, Selling or Merging
Your Accounting, Consulting or Tax Practice

Successful
PRACTICE SALES

The Complete Guide to
Buying, Selling or Merging
Your Accounting, Consulting or Tax Practice

John R. Ezell, CPA, and Ken Berry

Professional Horizons, Inc.
5050 El Camino Real, Suite 114
Los Altos, CA 94022
www.prohorizons.com

This book was edited and designed by:
The Roberts Group
12803 Eastview Curve
Apple Valley, MN 55124
www.editorialservice.com

ProHorizons and its logo are trademarks of Professional Horizons, Inc.

ISBN 0-7795-0097-0

Printed in Canada

CONTENTS

1. Introduction   1

An Industry in Transition   2
Practice Continuation Agreements   4
About This Book   4

2. Acquiring a Firm   7

Who Buys Accounting or Tax Firms?   8
Why Buyers Buy   9
Should I Buy?   10
The Buying Process   16
Why Do Some Deals Fall Apart?   27
Why Should a Buyer Consult a Broker?   27
Final Thoughts on Acquiring a Firm   29
Appendix Resources   29

3. Selling Your Practice   31

Who Sells Accounting or Tax Firms?   32
The Sales Process   33
Common Misconceptions about Buyers and Their Motivations   49
How Long is the Process? When Do You Need to Start?   51
Why Should a Seller Consult a Broker?   52
Final Thoughts on Selling Your Practice   53
Appendix Resources   54

4. Merger Considerations   **57**

Why Are There So Few True Accounting Practice Mergers?   57
Contemplating a Merger   59
Preparing for a Merger   61
Steps to Negotiating a Merger   64
Pitfalls Unique to Merging   65
Merger Checklist   67
Final Thoughts on Mergers   69

5. Financing an Acquisition   **71**

How Are Deals Financed?   72
Our Philosophy About Financing   75
Financing Considerations for the Buyer   76
Steps to Financing Your Acquisition   77
Lending Sources and Issues   78
Preparing Required Documents   80
Loan Approval   82
Timing   83
Final Thoughts on Financing   83

6. Life Cycle of a Sale   **85**

Independent Action Milestones   87
Initial Contact Milestones   90
Transaction Milestones   92
Transition Milestones   95
Final Thoughts on the Sales Life Cycle   96

7. Land Mines, Pitfalls and Issues to Avoid   **97**

Selling Your Practice for Too Little   97
Wasting Time on Unqualified Buyers   100
Selling to the Wrong Buyer   101
Settling on Unsatisfactory Terms or Contingencies   101
Not Planning for Sufficient Client Loss   103
Breaching Confidentiality   105
Automatically Selling to an Employee or Partner   107
Focusing on One Buyer   109
Waiting Too Long to Sell   109
Conducting Insufficient Due Diligence   110
Being a Lone Ranger   111
Final Thoughts on Land Mines, Pitfalls, and Issues to Avoid   115

8. In Closing   117

Set Your Goals and Make a Plan   117
Understand the Process and Implement It   118
Do Not Become Overwhelmed and Bogged Down   119
Maintain a Positive Outlook   119
Beware the Many Pitfalls   120
Additional Information   120
Contacting the Author   120

Appendix A: Internet Resources   121

Appendix B: Sample Documents   123

Sample Letter of Intent   124
Sample Letter: Seller Announcing Sale to Clients   126
Sample Letter: Buyer Introduction to Clients   127
Sample Confidentiality Agreement   129

Appendix C: Due Diligence Checklist   131

Sample Due Diligence Analysis   134

Appendix D: State Boards of Accountancy   137

Appendix E: State Societies and Associations   149

State EA Societies   149
State CPA Societies and Associations   156

General Business Acquisition Terms   167

Index   189

CHAPTER ONE

Introduction

Some of my colleagues and competitors think this book is a crazy idea. They think I am going to diminish the client pool for the tax and accounting brokerage industry. That it will create more "for sale by owner" situations. That I am going to cannibalize my prospective clients and theirs. My response to them is simple— "You are not hearing what I am hearing."

Every month I talk with someone who has been, or is, in a legal battle resulting from a "for sale by owner" practice sale or acquisition. The money spent on legal fees and time concerning this type of litigation is incredible! If it is not someone in a legal battle, it is someone who is exploring the idea of a new broker because his existing broker has been inactive on the practice sale and he has not seen the results he expected.

My goal with this book is to address these two conversations with the knowledge and expertise I have gained over the past ten years as an accounting practice broker and over the past fourteen years as a certified public accountant (CPA)—sixteen years in the

CPA industry. First, I want to equip those who are determined to sell on their own with a basic level of information. It is critical that you implement a process and understand what you are undertaking if you are to protect yourself while pursuing a "win-win" agreement with the other party.

Then, for those who plan to pursue a sale or acquisition through an intermediary, my goal is for this book to be a guideline for the seller or buyer. With a model process in hand and an understanding of what steps could be taken, you will be better equipped to evaluate whether your broker is truly working for you. Unfortunately, there is an increasing number of brokerage operations that are little more than Internet listing agents gleaning a percentage of the final sales price with little value added. With this book in hand, I hope that you will be able to discern the value-added brokers from the rest and reach your goal of selling or buying a firm in an acceptable manner, for a fair value, and in a reasonable amount of time.

An Industry in Transition

The goals I mentioned above need to be understood against the backdrop of an industry in change. Twenty years ago, buying or selling a practice was a pretty straightforward affair—an owner would find a younger CPA and hand over the practice for a small percentage of the fees during the following five to ten years. Today, the buying market is dramatically different.

There are public companies entering the market, large traditional firms swallowing smaller firms, independent firms combining to become larger firms, and younger professionals acquiring their first practices. The entire profession is changing or has changed in the past decade. As I write this, American Express, the original accounting industry consolidator, has announced it is spinning off its financial advisory services so it can focus on its faster growing credit card and travel services. I guess it is going back to its roots.

Now offshore outsourcing firms have sprung up, and firms are electronically sending information to be processed overseas. A firm can send tax return data to an overseas processing center and, for as little as $30 to $50, it can have draft returns back in eighteen to twenty-four hours. This is work that used to take days to process and would often require hiring additional seasonal staff. Accounting has become a dynamic business.

From the buyer's perspective, these are challenging developments. The average accounting and tax firm will likely be larger in the future and require more capital, better managerial skills, and strong entrepreneurial instincts. With all these sales avenues available, it has truly become a seller's market. This ties into another conversation we increasingly have with buyers who are frustrated that they have not been able to acquire a firm of interest. A serious buyer can no longer afford to wait around and debate whether a practice is the perfect fit or delay in making an offer. Actively engaging a seller as soon as possible, even if you only have marginal interest, has become a crucial tactic. Handling the acquisition process with care and tact has never been more important. As a buyer, it is important to remember that sellers have many choices when it comes to transitioning their practice.

From the seller's perspective, your colleague down the street may no longer be the most qualified buyer for your practice. As a retiring practitioner, your friends and colleagues may be retiring themselves. You want a buyer who can sustain the work of the combined practices. Otherwise, during the first or second tax season, the buyer may find himself or herself unable to serve all of the clients and will show greatest loyalty to his or her longtime clients. The seller's former clients, feeling under-served, may drift away and find another accountant. This may jeopardize your final payout, possibly your final earnings. A qualified buyer is one with the talent, the desire, and the capital needed to succeed. A qualified buyer will have a plan to serve the volume of activity produced by combining the practices.

Practice Continuation Agreements

Another key issue our firm has identified is the lack of succession planning. Surviving spouses often contact our office for advice on this matter after the death of the owner operator. Unfortunately, it may be too late. No matter your age, seriously consider establishing a practice continuation agreement with a colleague. Plan now to protect your practice and your estate.

The value of most practices will deteriorate rapidly upon the owner's death or disability. Usually the spouse is not fully aware of what services are provided, their value, or even who the clients are.

This book is not intended to help in creating practice continuation agreements. However, it may be best to find a larger firm with which to enter into a practice continuation agreement. A larger firm may have the ability to more quickly and readily absorb your work.

The agreement should include a reasonable method of determining the value and how it will be paid. This is not a situation in which you will expect to realize the full market value of your practice. The goal is to create a sales contingency plan to assist your clients and help your family cope financially in case of disability or death.

Contact your state society for additional recommendations.

About This Book

Before I break down the idea and structure behind this book, I need to state a few caveats to the reader. I am not a professional writer. I am not an academic. What follows in these pages are my observations and knowledge gained from hands-on, real-life experience with the sale, acquisition, and merger of accounting and tax practices. The result, I believe, is a wealth of information in an easily digested format, although at times it is perhaps a bit rough.

As for the book's content—it has come out of a variety sources: notes I've taken regarding conversations with clients, articles I've written, content from the seminars I conduct, and, of course, the process and procedures we follow and the experiences we have at ProHorizons.

At this point, I would be remiss if I did not also acknowledge my gratitude to Leon Faris at Professional Accounting Sales. As the founder of Professional Accounting Sales, Mr. Faris is one of the pioneers of the intermediary business for accounting and tax firms. ProHorizons, in its early stage, was affiliated with Professional Accounting Sales and my knowledge and experience benefited from working alongside Mr. Faris.

Whether your goal is to buy, sell, or merge, you will discover useful information, examples, and case studies throughout this book. However, the content of this book and its structure are not to be considered definitive in regard to your sales, acquisition, or merger experience. Every transaction has unique issues, challenges, and steps, and should be handled accordingly. In this book, I am providing guidelines and milestones for a model transaction process.

The book breaks down and examines the sale and acquisition process from both the buyer's and seller's perspective. Chapter 2, *Acquiring a Firm*, and chapter 5, *Financing an Acquisition*, are addressed more to the buyer; while chapter 3, *Selling Your Practice*, is addressed more to the seller. The remaining chapters, *Merger Considerations*, *Lifecycle of a Sale*, and *Land Mines, Pitfalls and Issues to Avoid* are equally split between the perspectives and issues of both parties. This is not to say that if you are a seller you should not read chapters 2 and 5. To the contrary, we recommend you examine those chapters and gain a perspective on the issues, challenges, and processes the buyer will experience. This can only benefit you in navigating the sales process. Likewise, a buyer will benefit from understanding the seller's issues, challenges, and processes discussed in chapter 3.

When examples in this material refer to accounting practices, tax practices, or CPA firms, consider this as a general term to describe all types of accounting, tax, and financial service firms. When a reference is made to a type of practice, apply this to your own situation, whether it is a CPA firm, an enrolled agent (EA) practice, a non-certified tax preparation company, or a bookkeeping operation. While there are differences in operations or valuations, the overall sale and acquisition process is similar.

The sample forms and selected material from this book and from the appendix are available on our Web site at www.prohorizons.com/resources/forms. Use your last name as the login, enter your e-mail address, and enter the following password **B4US0BRT**. (The fifth character in the password is the number zero).

I hope you find this book useful and are able to use some of the content to enhance your transaction experience.

Regards,
John Ezell

Additional Acknowledgments

I wish to extend my greatest appreciation to several people. To Ken Berry, my co-author, without whose help and guidance this book would have never been possible. To my wife, Jennifer, without your loving support, balanced guidance, and editorial help, I'd probably be doing something entirely mundane. To Kevin Phillips, thanks for being my sounding board, mentor, and friend. To Marty Desmond, my great friend, Semper Fi! To my support staff, Regina, Sandra, Ruth, and the rest of the ProHorizons team, you are all terrific and I so value your support and insights. Thank you all!

CHAPTER TWO

Acquiring a Firm

Buying a practice is serious business and should not be undertaken lightly. Everyone has different reasons for choosing business ownership. Whether you seek a change in lifestyle with more personal freedom and profit potential, the expansion of current business, or any number of motivations, it is important that any potential acquisition match your individual interests, goals, and capabilities. This chapter will help prepare you for a successful transition in the new opportunity.

Frequent Questions on Buying

Thinking about buying a practice? More and more people are considering the acquisition of an existing practice to reach their career objectives. Below are some questions entrepreneurs frequently ask in this situation:

- How are practices valued?
- Should an attorney be consulted when buying a practice?
- Is it better to buy an existing business or to start a new business?

- When should due diligence be performed?
- How long should due diligence take?
- Should the transaction be a stock or asset sale?
- What is a business broker and should one be consulted?
- Who does the broker represent?
- What are the benefits of utilizing a broker?
- How can I find the right type of practice?
- Why do practices seem to sell before I get a chance to review them?
- Should I get prequalified for financing?
- Why do deals fall apart?
- What is involved in the transition process?

Who Buys Accounting or Tax Firms?

There are principally three types of buyers—individual buyers, synergistic buyers, and financial buyers.

The Individual Buyer: The individual buyer category encompasses a variety of buyer types including wealthy individuals, corporate financial executives, and accountants and tax professionals working for other firms. This category represents the largest number of prospective buyers but not necessarily actual buyers of small to mid-size firms.

The Synergistic Buyer (corporate/strategic buyers): Synergistic buyers are established partnership or sole proprietor firms within a geographic market. This buyer's primary goal is to acquire a firm or a group of firms within the same geographic area to gain economies of scale and business growth not otherwise available. Consolidators may also fall into this category.

The Financial Buyer: Financial buyers seek to acquire an accounting or tax firm as an investment because of the high profit potential or the ability to expand the offerings of a professional services company. Financial buyers are typically large consolidators, such as CBIZ (Century Business Services), American Express, HRB Business Services, or Fiducial (the owner of Triple Check and Comprehensive Business Services). However, the individual buyer looking at owning a practice more as an investment than a job would also fall into this category.

We'll look more closely at these types as we discuss some of the reasons for acquiring practices.

Why Buyers Buy

Why should someone buy an existing practice rather than start one? For starters, an existing practice has a track record and can usually generate income to begin offsetting the initial investment from the first day of acquisition. Successful practices tend to be those that have been stable and profitable for several years.

> **Is it better to buy an existing business or to start a business?** There are many advantages to acquiring an existing practice, but the reduced risk of failure is usually the most compelling. An existing practice has an established track record and client base and provides immediate cash flow.

Some advantages to buying an existing practice rather than a start-up include:

- Actual results rather than proforma
- Immediate cash flow
- Trained employees in place
- Established clients and referral sources
- Existing facilities and operations
- Training by the seller
- Availability of financing

Whatever the reasons, you should buy a practice that you enjoy and would feel comfortable running. Aspiring to be your own boss and calling your own shots may seem lofty, but it is attainable. The types of practices you explore should fit these objectives.

Should I Buy?

The Individual Buyer

Both personal and professional skills are required to run a successful practice. There should be some introspection into personal traits and principles to evaluate your skills. Keep in mind all of the people this decision affects, including family, friends, colleagues, and future employees. Ask yourself:

- How is my family situation? Will acquiring a practice require a change of lifestyle such as relocation? What about the hours involved and their impact on relationships? Will family members be involved in operations? How will this change the dynamics of existing relationships?

- Am I financially prepared for this process? Purchasing a practice typically requires loans, and depending on the cash flow, returns on the investment may take some time to materialize.

- Do I trust my instincts? The most successful entrepreneurs are people with the ability to identify gut reactions. They're able to rely on their instincts and capitalize on opportunities. They pay attention to the numbers but aren't bogged down solely in figures. They know how to market and grow, but they don't overanalyze every situation.

- What about my commitment level? Most practitioners are used to working long, hard hours during tax season. How is your stamina for the long haul? Most entrepreneurs have a mission for integrating their professional lives with their personal values. Thus, they are highly motivated, responsible, and have a sense of pride and ownership. They know and accept that the overall success of their businesses is their own responsibility.

Buy Versus Build

Depending on your personality and practice development ability, it is almost always better to buy a practice rather than build one from scratch. The following illustrates an example assuming the following:

- Purchasing a practice grossing $350,000 with 50% profit, 5% annual growth, 100% financed, and the buyer provides the working capital. (We believe these are realistic assumptions.)

- Building from a base of $100,000 and 20% annual growth, which is reduced to 5% annual growth when $350,000 gross is reached (same as purchase example); 65% profit is achieved until year 5, then reduces to 50% profit (same as purchase example); spending is consistent with additional marketing costs of $25,000 annually. (We believe these are relatively aggressive assumptions.)

Buying	10 years	Building	10 years
Gross	$ 4,402,262	Gross	$ 2,421,188
Expenses	$ 2,515,579	Expenses	$ 1,130,074
Net Profit	$ 1,886,684	Net Profit	$ 1,291,114
Debt Service	$ 594,750	Additional Marketing exp.	$ 250,000
Net Available for Buyer	$ 1,291,934	Net Available for Builder	$ 1,041,114
Buying over Building	**$ 250,820**		

- How are my problem-solving skills? Am I adept at identifying issues and creating and implementing solutions? Is there a strong network of colleagues and friends to provide advice, encouragement, and support as the practice grows? Entrepreneurs need to look at the total picture, seeing problems as opportunities rather than roadblocks.

- Am I decisive as well as resilient? Stuff happens. Sometimes crises and setbacks occur. Running a small business will require you to make a variety of decisions regarding personnel issues as well as marketing and client issues. Being agile and decisive can help you make the changes necessary to put out fires and keep things moving to take advantage of new opportunities.

- Do I take initiative? Can I work independently? Am I able to appraise and take advantage of situations? Entrepreneurs seize opportunities as they arise and make things happen. Are you willing to take risks to reap rewards?

- What is my enthusiasm level? Do I deal tactfully with people, especially in stressful situations? Do I have the ability to separate my role/position from my identity? Self-confidence is integral to running a business. You will need to feel confident of the decisions you make, sometimes under pressure. Can you focus on the big picture, turning problems into opportunities? Can you listen to employees and clients without becoming defensive?

- Do I have the courage to try new things, and am I willing to make mistakes? Managing a practice means that mistakes will happen. Am I willing to accept responsibility and tackle the challenges directly? Can I learn from my mistakes and accept feedback as I develop my leadership skills?

- How open-minded am I? Am I receptive to advice? Do I try to make decisions in a vacuum, or do I seek advice from others? Do I seek support and guidance when I need it?

Specific abilities and experience are vital to the success of a practice. You may discover that you do not have all of the necessary skills or the time to accomplish everything, and you'll need to hire personnel to cover any deficiencies. At this point, ask yourself:

Opportunity
Combining your current practice with another larger practice or taking a role with ownership possibilities may help fulfill your long-term goals. We uncover several opportunities each year for this type of arrangement.

- Do I understand the basic functions and skills needed to run a successful practice?

- Do I have those skills?

- Do I have practice development skills?

- Can I obtain new clients to replace clients lost?

- How strong are my management or supervisory skills? What experience do I have in this function?

- What experience do I have in this type of practice?

- What professional training prepares me for this?

- What are my experiences in recruiting, hiring, and growing a staff? Can I determine if the applicants' skills meet the requirements for the positions I'll be filling?

You may discover that you need to develop some of the skills needed to own a practice. Perhaps the personal commitment is more than you can reasonably make at this time. Are you willing to delay your plans until you have acquired the necessary experience? Would you consider working with a partner? Would taking a role in another firm be beneficial in expanding your capabilities?

The Synergistic Buyer (Corporate/Strategic Buyers)

Many times the desired practice may offer unique market share not previously available to the acquiring firm. Often buyers are seeking to add services not previously provided but synergistic to their existing client base. (We saw this several years ago with consolidations by CBIZ, American Express, HRB Business Services, etc.) The firm should ask:

- Are we making this acquisition to acquire people, increase profits, expand market share, or broaden geographic coverage?

- How will the acquired practice add to existing technical expertise, services, clientele, etc.?

- Will the services, specializations, and talents of the target firm be a synergistic fit?

- Will the services of the target firm be a good fit with our client base?

- Do we have the time to attend to the acquisition and the acquired clients personally?

- How will the clients react to the acquisition?

- How compatible are the billing structures and compensation levels of the two firms?

- How compatible are the organizational cultures of the two firms?

- Can the staff of the target firm be integrated with our own staff?

- Have key personnel been identified, and are they expected to stay on with the new firm?

- Will the acquisition affect referral sources?

The Financial Buyer

The financial buyer is not buying a job but is making an investment. Ask yourself:

- Why do I want to buy an accounting practice?

- Do I wish to be an active or passive part of the new firm?

- Do I have the entrepreneurial and technical skills required?

- Is this the specific type of practice that I am interested in purchasing?

- What is the minimum income required from a business to meet my expectations and existing commitments?

- What is my preference regarding location?

- What is the maximum amount of funds I will invest as a down payment?

Example of a Financial Buyer

Our firm sold a large tax preparation firm to a buyer who had limited tax preparation experience but had built and run a successful real estate brokerage. The seller was willing to stay on as an employee for a couple of years. The practice had a number of tax preparers, and the buyer had experience managing people. Obviously, there were hurdles in the deal, but the buyer was willing to make a large down payment and secure the note with real estate, significantly reducing the risk to the seller. The buyer looked at owning and running this business more as an investment than buying a job. The buyer was satisfied with the results, and, three years later, we assisted him with another acquisition.

The Buying Process

Decision to Grow, Expand, Relocate

The idea of buying a practice is usually the result of professional decisions, although personal life factors may come into play. On the professional side, you may be looking to grow by adding talented staff, adding new services, acquiring competition, acquiring new clients, expanding into new territory; or you may be simply beginning or building your first practice. On the personal side, you may be looking to relocate in order to change your environment or reduce your cost of living. It is usually a chain of events and thoughts that leads to the decision to buy—slow business development leads to increased need for new clients, which leads to the idea of acquiring new clients, which leads to the decision to buy an existing practice.

Determine Type of Practice Being Sought

The decision to buy a practice may dictate some of the criteria of the practice being sought—location, staff in place, services offered. It is important to determine the size of the practice both in regard to cash flow or earning potential and in regard to number of clients. Finding the right balance between positive growth and overwhelming workload is important. Introspective awareness of your own skills—management, technology, interpersonal and business development skills—will help you define criteria that match your capabilities.

Search Market for Practices that Meet Criteria and Make Inquiries about Practices of Interest

With your criteria established, you can begin to search the market for practices of interest. Start by checking local or state association newsletters, industry periodicals, local newspapers, and brokerage Web site listings.

Some resources you should utilize in your search:

- Specialized accounting firm brokers (our firm, ProHorizons, for example)

- General business brokers (not as strong a source as specialty brokers)

- Professional organizations, associations, and state societies

- *Journal of Accountancy*

- State society newsletters or Web sites (an excellent source)

- Newspaper classifieds

- *Wall Street Journal* classifieds

- Internet (www.prohorizons.com, www.bizbuysell.com, www.aicpa.org, state society Web sites)

When you find a practice of interest, make an immediate inquiry, get answers to your initial questions, and verify how serious the seller is about selling.

Present Your Skills, Qualifications, and Level of Interest

Provided both parties are interested, there will be follow-up conversations after your initial inquiry. It is important to use these opportunities for more than information gathering. Be sure to present yourself, your capabilities, and your interest when appropriate. The seller will be weighing much more than finances in choosing a buyer.

Receive Business Sales Memorandum and Look into Financing

The business sales memorandum (see pages 42–43 for definition) provides you with your first look into the details of the practice for sale. Use this document as an initial measure of the fit with your purchase criteria and goals. If the practice is still appealing, you should set the mechanisms of acquisition into motion by arranging a meeting with the seller and possibly looking into any loan or financing assistance you may need.

> **Should I get prequalified for financing before buying a practice?** If there is a high demand for a practice being sold, the most qualified buyers tend to go to the head of the line. A major part of being qualified is proving that financial resources are available to complete the transaction.

Meet with Seller and Visit Practice Location

The buyer/seller meeting is an important step. Remember the adage about first impressions. To a large degree, the success of this meeting will depend on your ability to connect with the seller. The seller has invested both financially and emotionally in the practice and wants to ensure that it is sold to an individual who will care about the practice and the clients.

There are several intangible fundamentals to a successful meeting. These factors influence the way you are perceived and will affect the degree of rapport you establish with the owner.

- **Enthusiasm**—Leave no doubt as to your level of interest in this opportunity. You may think this is unnecessary, but sellers often choose the more enthusiastic candidate in the case of a tie. It is best to keep your options open— wouldn't you rather be in a position to decline submitting an offer than have a prospective purchase evaporate from your grasp?

- **Technical competence and interest**—Sellers look for people who love what they do and are excited by the prospect of applying their expertise to a given project.

- **Confidence**—A buyer who demonstrates his or her strengths and accomplishments will be more favorably received.

- **Questions**—You learn more by asking questions than talking. Ask the seller about the business, his or her interests, and what characteristics he or she is looking for in a buyer.

- **Intensity**—The last thing you want to do is come across as "flat" in your presentation. There's nothing inherently wrong with being relaxed, but present yourself with energy and interest.

> **Confidentiality**
>
> Please remember to keep all proprietary information obtained about the practice confidential. Only discuss this information with those covered by any executed confidentiality agreement, and remind them that the information is confidential in nature. In most cases, the employees, clients, suppliers, landlords, and lenders are unaware of the sale and premature disclosure could have a negative impact. (See appendix B for a sample agreement.)

- **Professional expertise**—Provide a current résumé which presents your background and skills in a thorough and accurate manner.

- **Research**—Gather current information regarding the company, its competitors, and its market positioning to assist in your decision.

> **How is fair market value of a business determined?**
> This is a complex issue. In general, business values are determined by a combination of the value of the underlying assets' values and a capitalization of normalized profits. CPA and EA firms are generally priced at a multiple of gross revenues starting at one times gross.

Make a strong case for why the seller should choose you by providing evidence of your professional competence and skills. Build rapport and sell yourself as the ideal buyer.

Never leave a meeting without exchanging fundamental information. The more you know about each other, the more potential you'll have for establishing rapport and making an informed decision.

> **Note:** If institutional financing is required, and it usually is, a business broker can usually recommend various lending sources depending upon the type of financing needed. For more on financing, see chapter 5.

Conduct Pre-Offer Financial Review

Assuming a successful meeting in combination with sincere and mutual interest, you will need to decide two things: whether the opportunity fits your goals and, if so, what sort of offer to submit. It is normal to request additional financial information prior to making an offer. In requesting information from the seller for your pre-offer review, be sure to examine just the level of information you require to form a comfortable offer. Trying to uncover too much too early may make the seller question your motives and sour the deal. Once you have examined any requested information and are satisfied by the findings, make an offer. Finding a practice is difficult, and delay may result in a missed opportunity.

Information Requested for Pre-Offer Financial Review

The exact type and nature of the information requested varies from review to review. Below are some examples of the type of information typically requested:

● Three years of income statements or tax returns

● Summary of current lease terms

● Summary of revenue sources (i.e., write-up, tax preparation, bookkeeping, etc.)

● Employee information, compensation, tenure, billings

Make an Offer

The next step is to prepare a letter of intent to purchase. It should include the key elements of price and terms, fixed assets, non-compete clauses, transition issues, and a proposed closing date. Our firm has found that dealing with these five items up front will save a lot of time and misunderstanding later.

 Sample Document

A sample letter of intent is located in appendix B.

Should it be a stock or asset sale? Although each transaction is different, nearly all buyers acquire the assets of an existing practice, rather than the stock of the corporation being sold. This is primarily because of tax consequences and a desire to avoid assuming unknown liabilities.

Negotiate Terms and Conditions

The seller usually initiates negotiation of terms and conditions by sending a counteroffer or a request for clarification in response to the letter of intent. Both parties need to be careful about how they conduct negotiations. Having a solid understanding of the transaction process, the negotiable elements, and your role will help to smooth any bumps in this stage of the transaction.

Conduct Pre-Close Due Diligence

As in all business transactions, "caveat emptor" applies. Therefore, it is your responsibility to perform an adequate investigation prior to closing the sale to provide an inside view of the practice and corroborate the details of the valuation.

Once the deal parameters are finalized and financial resources verified, due diligence should be performed. The buyer can acquire great insight into the financial performance and operation through an office visit and discussion with the seller.

The specific review materials needed vary with

Taking a Leap of Faith

Regardless of how much due diligence you perform, regardless of how much advisors advise you, in the end you will be required to make some leap of faith to purchase a practice. There are no guarantees or sure things when it comes to buying a business. If you are not comfortable with the leap of faith required, you should not contemplate buying a business. The alternative to taking this leap of faith is commonly referred to as "analysis paralysis" and occurs when buyers get stuck in the due diligence phase of the acquisition process.

---

each situation and are up to the buyer's discretion. The review can be as intricate and involved as you require.

Due diligence on smaller practices may be completed in just a few hours. The time period may be much longer with larger, complicated acquisitions and may entail several different analyses.

Reviewing business records and issues can be time consuming for both parties. Furthermore, the buyer may incur costs for such things as professional advisors, copies of documents, lien searches, and closing documentation. An owner will not proceed without knowing that the buyer is serious and has made an acceptable offer. Therefore, before copies of tax returns and other business documents can be obtained and before any contact can be made with landlords, bankers, or advisors, proof of the buyer's financial ability and intent, as evidenced by an earnest money deposit and a letter of intent, must be accepted by the business owner.

> **Due Diligence by Lenders**
> Outside financing will also require due diligence. Lenders will ask for similar information to ensure the viability of the deal.

During the due diligence period, you should coordinate your request for documents with the seller and arrange meetings with related individuals including the owner's professional advisors, your professional advisors, the landlord, the lenders, the escrow attorney, and others as needed.

Sample Document

A sample due diligence checklist can be found in appendix C.

When you have completed the due diligence process and are satisfied with all aspects of the business, you will authorize your attorney to prepare the purchase agreement and other closing documents for the review and approval by all parties. A closing date is then scheduled. When involved, a broker coordinates with the principals and other necessary parties to ensure that all the required paperwork is completed by the closing date.

How long is the usual due diligence period for investigating a business after an offer has been made? It varies depending on the size and complexity of the deal. The normal period is between a few hours and a few days provided all of the material is ready for examination. This is all negotiable. Most sellers prefer a brief period to avoid disruption. There may also be other potential buyers, and they don't want to keep the practice "off the market" unnecessarily. Have your team in place before you make an offer.

Create the Purchase Agreement

After executing the letter of intent, you will prepare the purchase agreement in conjunction with the due diligence process. Most brokers have boilerplate agreements to be used as a starting point. An attorney should review the agreement, which should include:

- Exact Names—Buyer/Seller
- Sale Items (client files, equipment, work in process)
- Office Lease
- Notice to Clients
- Excluded Items (A/R, A/P)
- Method to Collect and Remit A/R (even when not included in the sale)
- Seller Warranties
- Buyer Warranties
- Purchase Price Allocation
- Payment Terms
- Covenant Not to Compete
  - Client List
  - Geographic Location

- Transition Process

- Default

- Insurability—Buyer/Seller

- Transfer of Files (access for seller for necessary functions)

- Fees—Broker, Attorney

- Hold Harmless—Buyer/Seller

- Limitations (not responsible other party)

- Prepaid Clause

- Expenses (both ways)

- Use of Name and Phone Number

- Due on Sale Clause

Should you consult an attorney when buying a practice? Absolutely! Buying a practice is a complex transaction, and we advise all buyers and sellers to avail themselves of legal advice. Usually attorneys do not get called in until the buyer and seller have settled on terms. First, be sure the buyer and seller can agree on terms and formalize this agreement with a letter of intent of sale memorandum. This will help focus the attorneys' attention on the agreement and not the deal negotiations. Attorneys are used to drafting and reviewing contracts and preparing closing documents with appropriate protection for the parties involved. In selecting an attorney, be sure to retain one with prior experience in business transfers.

Close the Transaction

Once all parties have agreed to the purchase agreement, there is an excellent chance that the transaction will be completed. However, there must be an end to the negotiation process for things to be finalized. At this point, the deal is still fragile with many components contingent on some other part of the agreement. Renegotiating points previously agreed upon can turn the other party off and lead to a collapse of the entire deal.

In addition to the purchase agreement, the following will be presented at the closing:

- Promissory note

- Bill of sale

- Wire transfer or a check

Meet the Staff and Introduce Yourself to the Acquired Clients

It's time to meet the staff. They will be concerned about their situation and anticipated changes to their individual roles and responsibilities as well as changes in the

> **Rule of Thumb**
> Smooth transactions make successful transitions.

workplace and operations. Be honest and straightforward; explain any changes in direction you have in mind.

The clients should be notified as soon as possible regarding the sale of the practice. A combination of meetings, phone calls, and mailings should be used to announce the sale and introduce the buyer. A strong focus should be put on pledging a continuation of the quality services provided for the same or similar fees, in addition to any new services, capabilities, or announcements.

Sample Documents

Sample letters for notifying clients are located in appendix B.

Transition the Practice

With the announcements and introductions to staff and clients taken care of, it will be important to notify vendors and business partners and align the organization under the buyer's management. This may require redefinition of personnel assignments, policies, and processes, as well as the seller's training the buyer in the existing client structure and service offering. Don't be in a hurry to hang "Under New Management" signs, but make the appropriate changes carefully.

Why Do Some Deals Fall Apart?

Many times, the buyer and seller reach a tentative agreement only to have it fail for various reasons. Once understood, most of the worst deal killers can be prevented. Both parties must identify and develop acceptable solutions.

What prevents a successful conclusion? See chapter 7, *Land Mines, Pitfalls and Issues to Avoid*, for an in-depth look at the most common problems encountered.

I've been looking for a long time. When I find the right practice, it seems as though there is a sale pending before I get any information. What can I do differently? It is important to stay highly involved in a search for a practice. This is currently a seller's market. There are many more buyers in the market than practices available. You must be ready to act quickly if you find a practice that meets your specifications. Ensure you have your financial resources ready, and be prepared to make a competitive offer on a suitable practice. Be a proactive buyer.

Why Should a Buyer Consult a Broker?

Unlike the sale of real property, a practice owner does not place a "for sale" sign on the lawn in order to preserve confidentiality with clients, staff, and competitors. Consequently, buyers may have difficulty identifying potential sales listings. Brokers represent numerous practices of different types and sizes. Additionally, as a result of the volume of transactions that brokers complete, they usually have a variety of financing contacts available to provide options for obtaining the most competitive financing package.

As part of the process of marketing a business, a professional broker will:

- Qualify sellers for motivation and review expectations and goals.

- Prepare a comprehensive business report.

- Provide a systematic process for both buyer and seller.

- Assist in the preparation of a realistic letter of intent.

- Manage problems as they arise and identify the appropriate resources, and provide the expertise to recognize and resolve issues between differing viewpoints.

When you speak with a business broker, be prepared to discuss your background, work experience, and financial ability to purchase a business. This information helps the broker identify potential practices that fit your goals. You should prepare a résumé and financial statement that will be required by lenders, landlords, and others who will be a party to the transaction.

Based on your qualifications and acquisition criteria, a broker will review appropriate practices with you. Profiles that contain a summary of the business and financial information will be provided after you sign a confidentiality agreement, which is required by the business owner.

A business broker will answer any additional questions you may have about the practices or will obtain the answers from persons deemed reliable. Once you select those practices that best meet your investment criteria, the business broker will schedule appointments with the owners so you can tour the offices and discuss the firms.

Final Thoughts on Acquiring a Firm

In this chapter, we examined the elements of an acquisition from several perspectives: types of buyers, reasons to buy, buying versus building, and questions you should ask if you are thinking about buying. We also went through a comprehensive model of the buying process, briefly touched on the reasons deals fall apart, and mentioned the value a broker brings to the process.

In regard to the buying process presented in this chapter, we explored the steps in a model acquisition. It is our hope that this will give you a rough road map of what to expect. However, you need to also recognize that the steps discussed may or may not be applicable to your situation. We have been involved with hundreds of transactions, and no two have been alike.

If we can leave you with a final thought on this chapter, it is that a positive outlook is crucial. We can highlight four elements that are mentioned and that are key components in completing a successful business transaction:

- Good rapport with all parties involved

- A mutual understanding of the terms of the agreement

- A mutual awareness of the roles and emotions of both the buyer and seller

- Belief that all parties are committed to a good transaction and a successful transfer

Appendix Resources

A few appendix resources for the buyer were mentioned in this chapter. Most notably:

- A sample letter of intent, found in appendix B

- A sample letter of introduction to clients, also found in appendix B

- A sample confidentiality agreement, also found in appendix B

- A sample due diligence checklist, found in appendix C

For Buyers

1. There are no "perfect" practices—do not expect to find one.

2. If, after reviewing information on an acquisition, it appears of even marginal interest, schedule a meeting with the owner. You always learn more when visiting with the owner and touring the office.

3. Ask anything and everything. There are no stupid questions.

4. Picture yourself as the owner of the practice under consideration and consider how it can be improved.

5. If you find a practice you like, make an offer based on your valuation and risk assessment.

6. Act decisively! Delaying an offer may result in a missed opportunity.

7. If other investors will participate, secure specific commitments as to expectations, and maintain their involvement throughout the process.

8. Make sure your acquisition criteria are realistic. Establish that you have sufficient cash to invest to purchase the practice (size and type) you desire.

9. Maintain a prudent reserve for unanticipated working capital requirements.

10. Identify and utilize advisors with experience in "deal-making." Their knowledge and expertise with these types of transactions will reduce the likelihood of anticipated delays and fees.

CHAPTER THREE

Selling Your Practice

Selling a practice is a difficult and emotional decision. While each seller has different motivations, most have similar goals for the outcome. These include financial rewards and the satisfaction of finding a talented successor to take care of their clients, some of whom have also become good friends. This chapter highlights the challenges that this career transition entails.

Frequent Seller Questions

- Is it a good time to sell?
- What is my practice really worth?
- How do I make my practice more valuable?
- How will I find the best buyers for my practice?
- How long will it take to sell my business?
- Is my practice ready for sale?
- What affects the selling price?
- How will I keep the process confidential?
- Will I need to carry part of the note?
- Do I need a business plan?

- What is a business broker?
- Why should I use a business broker?
- How will my business be advertised?
- What is my role in selling a business?
- Can you sell my business?
- How are negotiations handled?
- What is the closing process?

Who Sells Accounting or Tax Firms?

The average CPA or EA practice is really not very large. A review of a nationwide survey places the average firm revenue somewhere around $250,000 to $350,000 in gross, with two to four full-time employees and one owner. Our discussions with hundreds of practitioners every year support these findings, although we often assist firms several times that size.

Every firm will either sell, merge, or be disposed of in a lifetime and most likely to another individual owner. The reasons vary but usually involve:

- Retirement—full or semi-retirement
- Relocation
- Career change
- Hired by a client
- Burnout or wear out
- Work/life balance
- Health issues
- Spouse/partner/self seriously ill

The Sales Process

Decision to Retire, Relocate, or Change Careers

As mentioned previously, the idea of selling your practice is usually the result of one of these personal decisions. These decisions may be driven by age, wealth, environment, health, or some other personal life factor. In essence you have a chain of events and thoughts leading to your decision to sell. For example, too much work leads to too much stress, which leads to a desire to change careers, which leads to the decision to sell your practice.

> **The most common factors driving the decision to sell:**
> - Business risks creating stress
> - Health or worries about death or disability
> - Retirement
> - Relocation
> - Change in owner's desires, decision to pursue other business interests

Evaluate Your Practice, Establish a Relationship with a Broker or Intermediary, and Strengthen any Weaknesses

This is the process of sizing up your practice. Where are you strong and where are you weak—services, staff, clients, revenue, expenses, cash flow, etc.? At this point, it is wise to establish a relationship with a broker or intermediary. This will provide you with a fresh, objective set of eyes for evaluating your practice, as well as the expertise of knowing where to look and what to look for. A specialized accounting firm broker is knowledgeable about the market and the factors that motivate buyers to buy. Through the evaluation process, you will compile the data needed to determine the practice value. In addition, analysis of any practice weaknesses may provide some quick fixes that will strengthen the practice and increase the value.

Questions You Should Ask Yourself

- What type of practice do you have?
- Is your office location desirable?
- What are the factors and their priorities in your sales decision?
- How are your business numbers and do they generate a profit?

Determining Your Next Steps:

- Can you make short- or long-term adjustments to market your practice more effectively?
- Should you wait and sell your practice at a later date?

In some instances it may make sense to postpone the sale; in other cases, the process should begin immediately.

Conduct a Market Review

Identifying and analyzing market variables helps identify the competitive position of your practice. Preparing a business plan may help a prospective buyer to understand your business and its goals.

Questions to Ask in Preparation of Your Plan

- Is your market area growing or declining?
- Are any of your competitors interested in expanding?
- How much is your practice worth today?
- What are your retirement goals, and what will it take to reach them?
- Do you know how to identify and qualify potential candidates?
- What plans and procedures are in place if the unexpected happens to you?
- What factors are prospective buyers utilizing in business acquisitions?
- Do you have a plan to transfer the business to a successor, and do you have the expertise to implement that process successfully?

Buyers consider a variety of criteria in the decision to purchase, especially the practice's ability to make money. The more profitable practice will usually generate higher selling prices and sell more quickly. Buyers also concentrate on cash flow, growth, and stability. Value-building strategies should match your specific goals.

- Many businesses generate significant cash revenue that should be reported. Most buyers won't pay for unreported funds, and banks will not finance a transaction without a strong cash flow.

- Identify "owner perks" to show real profitability. Accurate demonstration will help lenders accept these adjustments and will create a higher sales price.

- Adjust fees based on your demonstrated worth and current market trends.

- Present your business as a clean opportunity with assets that are productive and provide the maximum investment return.

- Develop staff skills in key roles to enhance the desirability of your practice. Delegating responsibility reduces dependence on the owner and enables the buyer to focus on a smooth transition while other personnel effectively carry out day-to-day operations.

Set Price and Terms

Putting a price on their company is a challenge for all business owners. In addition to personal factors and the terms of the deal, there is a monetary concern. If the price is too high, buyers will not be interested; if the price is too low, sellers will not get the return they deserve.

Most buyers review the following criteria:

- **Debt**—Is the cash flow sufficient to cover the debt load used to acquire the practice?

- **Owner's Salary**—Does the practice generate enough income and a reasonable salary after expenses?

- **Replacement of Assets**—Is the practice income adequate to replace fixed assets as they are retired?

- **Return of Invested Capital**—After meeting the above criteria, is the return on invested capital commensurate with their perception of risk?

Other Details That Influence the Value of a Practice

- Location. Location. Location.
- Timing: quick sale vs. willingness to wait for the right price.
- Profitability—the more the better.
- "Beauty is in the eye of the beholder." Therefore, ultimately, the market and the buyers determine the price.
- Does the buyer *really* want your practice? Your colleague down the hall may just want "to look."
- Is the demand so strong for practices that buyers are willing to pay a premium?
- Is the demand so weak that the buyer is concerned about resale issues?

In addition to internal practice factors such as profitability and fee mix, other considerations that may affect the price include:

- Requiring a large down payment.
- Seeking a quick cash sale.
- Waiting for the highest price the market will bear.
- Pursuing a secure income stream.

Valuation and Deal Structure

There is a common misunderstanding in the accounting and tax industry that all practices are worth/valued one times annual billings. That number has been around so long many people, buyers and sellers, accept it as fact. It is not. Imagine comparing two practices with the same gross but vastly different net income. Is the one with the lower net income worth the same as the higher?

ARE THESE FIRMS BOTH WORTH $1,200,000?		
	Firm A	**Firm B**
Number of partners	2	2
Annual billable hours	2400	2800
Number of staff	4	6
Total annual staff billable hours	7200	9200
Firm-wide average rate per hour	$125	$100
Gross Billings	$1,200,000	$1,200,000
Expenses	$650,000	$850,000
Net income available for partners	$550,000	$350,000

We have seen variations on this hundreds of times. Value has more to do with supply and demand and profitability than gross revenues.

Structure of Transactions

There are many methods that may be used to value a business. Some are based on the earning power of the business such as the Capitalization-of-Earnings Method (net income/cost of capital = fair market value) and the Discounted-Future-Earnings Method. But for the accounting and tax industry there are four basic structures and valuation methods for purchasing accounting and tax practices.

Earn-outs

During an earn-out, a buyer agrees to pay a certain percentage of the billings over an established period of time. For example, a buyer agrees to pay 25 percent for five years. Some might conclude this total equals 125 percent of gross. This is not necessarily the case. The buyer argues that the seller will receive more money in time because fees will increase and services will expand, etc. Why would a buyer want to pay more money than necessary? The only logical reason is for the increased security provided by a five-year guarantee. In fact, under some of these arrangements, a buyer could change his mind with no additional liability.

Not all earn-outs are inappropriate, particularly when an earn-out is used as a portion of the final transaction value. For instance, an earn-out may be appropriate for internal buy-sell by partners or for remote locations. However, we have found that the simpler the structure the better the transaction's likelihood of success for all parties.

EXPECTED TRANSACTION—IDEAL EARN-OUT— REVENUE GROWTH

Gross collections of the selling firm equal $250,000. The parties agree to sales terms of 25% of collections for five years. At $250,000 average gross, that would appear to be a sales price of $312,500. However, one must look at the full five-year period.

	Collections	Payout @25%
Year 1	$250,000	$62,500
Year 2	$225,000	$56,250
Year 3	$250,000	$62,500
Year 4	$260,000	$65,000
Year 5	$270,000	$67,500
Total		$313,750
Present Value @ 6%		$270,000 approx.
Multiple of Average Gross		**1.08**

PROBABLE TRANSACTION—MORE LIKELY EARN-OUT— REVENUE DECLINE

Gross collections of the selling firm equal $250,000. The parties agree to sales terms of 25% of collections for five years. That would appear to be a sales price of $312,500. However, one must look at the full five-year period.

	Collections	Payout @25%
Year 1	$250,000	$62,500
Year 2	$225,000	$56,250
Year 3	$200,000	$50,000
Year 4	$180,000	$45,000
Year 5	$150,000	$37,500
Total		$251,250
Present Value @ 6%		$213,060 approx.
Multiple of Average Gross		.85

Seller beware! This is a scenario most buyers consider and most sellers overlook. When the annual payment structure fluctuates based on year-to-year results, the buyer is not accountable for maintaining activity on your business and, thus, has little motivation to perform. The seller incurs all of the risk with zero ability to affect the outcome. This is a classic "cherry-picking" scenario, where a buyer does not guarantee annual payments and has little intention of servicing more than the top percentage of your accounts.

Fixed Price

This is an easy method of structuring a sale. The buyer agrees to pay a fixed price, and the terms can be anywhere from all cash at closing to a 100 percent installment note. Few practices are sold this way, but maybe they should be. Nearly all other types of businesses are sold using this method. It may necessitate lowering the sales price, but most sellers would readily discount for a simple structure.

This approach also eliminates some of the difficulties of the transition period. Frequently, a seller worries that a buyer is not doing all that is required to successfully retain the clients. In such cases, the seller may feel the need to control the client contact.

However, a buyer must be free to establish solid client relationships.

Even the best transition plan will not retain 100 percent of the client base. Our observations suggest that some clients will see the transition as a time to make a change and select a new CPA. Plan for some client reduction regardless of the seller's or buyer's expertise, and you will encounter fewer surprises.

Multiple of Annual Gross Billings

Currently, this is the most common structure we utilize. The buyer and the seller agree to some multiple of annual gross billings, usually at some point between 100–150 percent of the annual gross. The annual period can be historical or for a future period. This method only makes sense with a future period; otherwise, a fixed price structure should be used. With a future period, there will be some process identified for how to calculate the "billing guarantee" and how an adjustment is made.

This method utilizes an approach of comparables to similar firms. It is a good approach that is heavily utilized in the industry despite the difficulty of obtaining relevant comparables. However, when too large a multiple is applied, buyers may not be interested. Another common mistake is to use the one times gross rule of thumb. As we illustrated earlier in this section, are two firms that each gross $1,200,000 worth an equal valuation when one nets $350,000 and the other nets $550,000? Probably not.

MULTIPLE ANNUAL GROSS TRANSACTION

Gross collections of the selling firm equal $250,000. The parties agree to sales terms of 125 percent of the buyer's first-year collections. The terms are 35 percent down ($110,000) and sixty monthly payments ($3,915) beginning three months after close with 6 percent interest. The sales price becomes $287,500.

	Collections	Payout—Approx.
Down Payment		$110,000
Year 1	$250,000	$31,320
Year 2	$205,000	$46,980
Year 3	$230,000	$46,980
Year 4	$250,000	$46,980
Year 5	$275,000	$46,980
Year 6		$15,660
Total		$344,900
Present Value @ 6%		$312,500
Multiple of Average Gross		**1.25**

In this model, we used the same numbers for collections that were used in the ideal earn-out model to demonstrate that, because of interest collection, this model surpasses even the best earn-out model. You could just as easily plug in the numbers of the more likely earn-out model, because the annual collections do not impact the payouts when using the multiple annual gross method. The buyer is responsible for paying based on first-year collections. So the buyer, not the seller, takes on the risk if the business is allowed to slide.

Net Income Multiples

This method also utilizes an approach of comparables to similar firms while also considering profit differences. It is a good approach which should probably be used more within the industry. This method guides a buyer comparing two or more acquisition candidates. Most small businesses, including CPA firms, sell for two to five times the net discretionary income.

Larger firms use this method when dealing with multiple owner transactions that involve several million dollars. The major consolidators in the industry also often use this method.

Other Methods Used Outside the Accounting and Tax Industry

Earnings Capitalization

This is a more theoretical approach typically used for larger businesses. The historical earnings (adjusted for discretionary items) are used in the following equation:

$$V = E/R$$

V= Valuation
E= Earnings Used
R= Capitalization Rate

Note that the capitalization rate varies for each buyer. For example, one may be happy with a 15 percent capitalization rate while another may require 30 percent.

Excess Earnings

This is another theoretical method used in valuing some closely held companies and is covered in more advanced business valuation manuals. In general, it is based on the premise that a buyer is entitled to a fair return on the investment in hard assets and that anything left over is excess earnings. A sales price is determined by an equation that takes a multiple of the value of hard assets combined with excess earnings.

Create a Comprehensive Business Sales Memorandum

With the completion of market research, pricing, and terms, a document describing your firm must be prepared which details all of the core aspects of your business and contains the information needed by a buyer to take the first step in acquisition.

At a minimum, the business sales memorandum should provide:

- Recasted financial statements.

- Summary of clients by number and type.

- Average fees per tax return.

- Lease terms.

> **Confidentiality**
> Maintaining confidentiality is an interlocking process that should be methodically practiced. Common sources of confidentiality breaches are:
> - Immediate family members
> - Bankers
> - Trusted friends
> - Employees and confidants

- List of job titles, tenure, compensation, billing, etc.

- Brief history of the firm and its owners.

- Acceptable price and terms—be realistic. This is not a time to be greedy, but you don't want to leave money on the table either.

Market the Sale of Your Practice

Find your buyers. Use your contacts and network to locate buyers. Consider placing advertisements on Web sites and in newspapers. Use direct mail to CPAs and EAs. Consider listing with a broker who specializes in accounting practices.

Identifying and working with multiple buyers increases your options when negotiating price and terms.

Field Inquiries Regarding Your Practice and Screen Buyers

Sellers should question buyers regarding their interest in acquiring the company. Try to determine the synergistic fit—you'll learn much more than you realize. Finding the right buyer is more important than the sales price and terms, especially if you are guaranteeing the revenue stream.

Assess how serious a prospect is about buying your practice, and then consider how the prospect will fit within the existing structure and environment. Some of the key concerns are:

- Is the prospect really interested in buying at this time?

- Does the prospect have the financial ability to purchase the business?

- Will clients and staff interact successfully with the prospect?

- Does the prospect have the professional competence to service your clients?

Without an intermediary, you will have to deal with each buyer through an extensive screening process. Some of these factors take time to uncover, and you do not want to discourage a prospect because you are too demanding. This process requires tact and diplomacy.

Evaluate Buyer Interest and Qualifications and Send Business Sales Memorandum

Based on your initial screening and the prospective buyers' presentations of their skills and interest, you will be able to isolate your serious prospects and take the next step toward closing the sale. Before sending the business sales memorandum, be sure the prospective buyers have received, signed, and returned confidentiality agreements.

Meet with Prospective Buyers

This is the first significant opportunity to size up your prospective buyers and take a significant step toward closing the sale. The buyer will arrive with many questions. Be sure to answer them, but don't forget to ask your own questions. Your goal is to determine whether you, your staff, and your clients can work with the prospective buyer, and whether you are comfortable with the buyer's level of enthusiasm, technical competence, and professional qualifications.

Provide Additional Information Necessary for Offers

Provided the meeting or meetings with a prospective buyer went well, the buyer should express interest in making an offer and may request additional information to assist in the formation of an offer. Information requested may include basic financials, a copy of your practice valuation, an estimate of annual client loss rate, and details regarding top account activity and trends. Be sure to protect critical proprietary information at this stage, such as your client list, and to avoid giving a buyer a "test drive" of your business.

> ### Information Requested for Pre-Offer Financial Review
>
> The exact type and nature of the information requested varies from review to review. Below are some examples of the type of information typically requested:
>
> - Three years of income statements or tax returns
> - Summary of current lease terms
> - Summary of revenue sources (i.e., write-up, tax preparation, bookkeeping, etc.)
> - Employee information, compensation, tenure, billings

Receive and Review Offers

A written offer should be submitted when a buyer is sufficiently interested in your practice. This offer may contain one or more contingencies, such as a detailed review of financial records, lease arrangements, or other pertinent business issues.

While an offer may be lacking in some areas, it should be carefully reviewed as it may include some terms worthy of serious consideration. It should include the key elements of price and terms, fixed assets, non-compete clauses, transition issues, and a proposed closing date. Our firm has found that dealing with these five items up-front will save time and will avoid misunderstanding later.

 Sample Document

A sample letter of intent is located in appendix B.

When considering multiple offers ask:

- Which prospect has the skills and abilities to continue the practice?
- Is the down payment large enough and are the terms adequate?
- Do the prospects have strong credit?

Answers to these questions and others will help you analyze the quality of each offer and decide which buyer to work with during the negotiation stage.

Negotiate Terms and Conditions

A counteroffer may be presented in response to the letter of intent or additional modifications may be requested. Now is the time to negotiate the details of the offer. A solid understanding of the transaction process and your role ensures no surprises.

Be cautious about renegotiating particular issues as this is a sign of a weak initial understanding or a planned manipulation of the deal. Nothing sours a deal more than having something changed when either party thought it had been finalized.

Provide Information for Pre-Close Due Diligence

As mentioned previously, buyers will want to perform due diligence and may bring in outside advisors to assist in reviewing the information. The seller should cooperate fully in this process lest the buyer think that the seller is hiding potential problems. Be open and provide details, but don't reveal every item about the business and its operation, especially the client list. Even at this stage of the process, beware of buyers seeking a "test ride."

When in agreement, both parties should work to satisfy and remove the contingencies in the offer. After all the conditions have been satisfied, final documents will be drafted.

Create the Purchase Agreement and Close the Transaction

A well-written agreement that spells out everything—price, terms, etc.—can be the difference between a deal that merely sounds good and a good deal that is enforceable.

A comprehensive purchase agreement covers:

- Exact Names—Buyer/Seller
- Sale Items (client files, equipment, work in process)
- Office Lease
- Notice to Clients
- Excluded Items—A/R and A/P (even if not included in the purchase)
- Method to Collect and Remit A/R
- Seller Warranties
- Buyer Warranties
- Purchase Price Allocation
- Payment Terms
- Covenant Not to Compete
  - Client List
  - Geographic Location

- Transition Process
- Default
- Insurability—Buyer/Seller
- Transfer of Files
- Fees—Broker, Attorney
- Hold Harmless—Buyer/Seller
- Limitations (not responsible other party)
- Prepaid Clause
- Expenses (both ways)
- Use of Name and Telephone Number
- Due on Sale Clause

Announce the Sale to Staff and Announce the Transition/Change to Clients

Avoid any sudden shifts or changes after closing the transaction. This eliminates additional stresses while employees and clients adjust to the change and become acquainted with the buyer. As soon as the transaction is closed, the seller should hold a meeting to announce the sale to the staff. Follow that meeting with a "meet the new owner" gathering for the the staff.

Key clients should be called as soon as possible after the sale is closed. A letter should be sent shortly after closing.

Transition procedures to follow:

- Notify the staff.
- Notify the clients.
- Prepare and send individual letters to clients, not an announcement. (See appendix for sample.)
- Introduce the buyer to the clients. Personal introductions are best, but not practical for all clients.
- Notify vendors.
- Train the buyer.

Sample Documents

Sample letters for notifying clients are located in appendix B.

Transition the Practice

With the announcements and introductions to staff and clients taken care of, it will be important to notify vendors and business partners and align the organization under the buyer's management. This may require redefinition of personnel assignments, policies, and processes, as well as the seller's training the buyer in the existing client structure and service offering.

Common Misconceptions about Buyers and Their Motivations

Money is the key motivator. A mistaken belief is that money is the key motivator in seeking to own a practice. Actually, if money is the main desire, a warning alarm should go off before you proceed. Most entrepreneurs go into business for themselves to run their own "show," be their own boss, and build something for themselves.

Be Careful Not to Self-Sabotage Your Sale

Do not accept work back from a client who says he does not want Joe Buyer's services and only wants to work with you, Sam Seller. Once that door is opened, it may be difficult to close. Of course, clients would prefer to work with the seller because a relationship has been established over the past several years.

Be firm when responding to the client, "Well, I knew it would be difficult for you to work with someone else, but I have decided to retire and turn over all my accounts to Joe Buyer. I trust that you will feel comfortable with Joe after you get to know him. In fact, you might find he is smarter than I am. I spent several months in this selection process in an effort to find the best possible CPA to serve my clients. I am sure you can understand my desire to retire and to begin the next phase of my life."

Studies indicate that money is important but somewhere in the middle of the list of reasons people give regarding their interest in business ownership.

If buyers aren't primarily money driven, then what are their motivations?

- A sense of pride in the service or product
- Control of their destiny
- Independence
- Flexibility
- Self-reliance
- Customer contact
- Earning potential—money
- Management potential
- Recognition
- Security
- Status

Buyers know the exact types of practices they want to buy. It's a faulty assumption that a prospective buyer knows from the start the exact kind of practice he or she wants to buy. Our experience has taught that what most buyers decide to purchase is usually different from what first caught their attention.

In determining the right practice for the right personality, here are some of the crucial questions a prospective buyer might ask:

- Does the practice intrigue me?
- Do I feel that my skills can enhance the performance of the practice?

- Would the practice offer "pride of ownership"?

- Would I feel content operating the practice?

A large local firm will be my best buyer. Many owners of successful practices think the best buyer for their firm is the large local firm. The problem with that assumption is twofold. First, if their business is

> **Buyers Adjust Their Criteria**
> We recently worked with a buyer who lived in the San Fernando Valley and, of course, wanted to buy a practice in the San Fernando Valley. Unfortunately, those practices are hard to acquire. There are many buyers in the valley, and few practices for sale. So when a practice became available in nearby Ventura County, he considered expanding his geographic area and went to look at it. Well, he loved the practice and submitted an earnest money deposit that same day. Being open to buyers outside your region will greatly expand your options in selling.

successful, the owners may not have a need or desire to acquire your practice. Second, our experience shows that many of the large local firms are not always willing to put "skin" in the game. They would be happy to have an acquisition that is on their terms, which may be little or no money down, resulting in the seller taking all the risk.

How Long is the Process? When Do You Need to Start?

If you want to sell before the next tax season, then consider beginning the process soon after the current season ends. This approach gives you an adequate amount of time to evaluate your goals, identify the best possible buyer, secure favorable terms, and complete the transition process.

The chart on the next page reflects when practice sales close. Remember most practices take three to six months, or longer, to

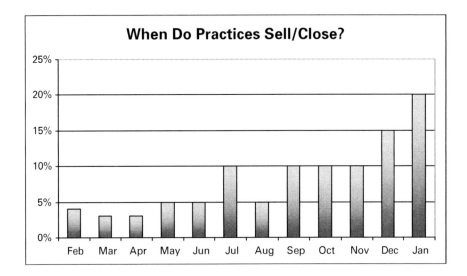

sell; so, you can estimate the start of the cycle by backing the figures up accordingly. Many sellers intend to start the process in April or May, but life gets in the way and they delay until November or December. The result: another tax season comes and goes before they are able to complete the sale of the practice.

Why Should a Seller Consult a Broker?

Whatever your size or goals, a competent intermediary will allow you to remain calm during what is sure to be a tense time. Sometimes personalities interfere with making good business decisions—you should have someone familiar with both parties with whom to discuss details. The intermediary can be an attorney, business broker, practice management consultant, or close business colleague.

A competent brokerage firm that specializes in handling accounting firms will not only be able to ask the buyer the tough questions and to represent your interest, it will also have a stable of prospective buyers that will give you enough candidates from which to choose the right buyer. A broker will save you much wasted time by screening potential buyers and only introducing those who are appropriate candidates. A broker will know who is or is not a candidate for your practice. Brokers will also stimulate demand and competition among motivated buyers, which increases the sales price.

While intermediaries receive a portion of the sales price, their experience in marketing, financing, negotiation, and the closing process provides valuable expertise and almost always secures a higher price than a "for sale by owner" deal. Thus, the intermediaries' fees are covered by the increased price and improved terms.

The value-added services of using a broker or intermediary include:

- The experience of many completed transactions
- Integrated marketing campaign to an established database of contacts
- Thorough screening of identified candidates before you meet any potential buyers
- Boilerplate agreements
- Consulting advice and availability as a sounding board
- Valuation expertise

Final Thoughts on Selling Your Practice

In this chapter, we examined the sale of a practice from several perspectives: who sells accounting and tax practices, common misconceptions about buyer motivations, how long a sale takes and when you should start the process, and the value a broker can bring to the process. We also presented a comprehensive breakdown of a model sales process and a variety of deal structure and valuation methods.

Similar to the previous chapter, it is our hope that the model sales process presented will give you a rough road map of what to expect. Keep in mind that no two transactions are alike. Apply the steps that are applicable to your situation.

Also as in the previous chapter, we would like to leave you with the final thought that positive outlook is crucial. Whether you are selling or acquiring a practice, the same components lead to a successful transaction:

- Good rapport with all parties involved

- A mutual understanding of the terms of the agreement

- A mutual awareness of the roles and emotions of both the buyer and seller

- Belief that all parties are committed to a good transaction and a successful transfer

Appendix Resources

A few appendix resources for the buyer were mentioned in this chapter. Most notably:

- A sample letter notifying clients of sale, found in appendix B

- A sample letter of confidentiality, also found in appendix B

- A sample due diligence checklist, found in appendix C

TOP 10
Tips

When Selling Your Practice

1. Follow a sales process and be prepared during all of its phases.

2. Maintain a "business as usual" attitude. Don't become distracted and lose clients.

3. Create competition by working with multiple buyers.

4. Negotiate with the goal of creating a successful outcome for both parties.

5. Keep things moving—time kills deals.

6. Consider a reasonable price range when offering your practice for sale.

7. Prepare a comprehensive profile of your practice prior to offering your practice for sale.

8. Be open-minded and professional in your dealings with buyers. Even if a buyer does not work out, he or she may refer one that will.

9. Don't forget to plan for a transition.

10. Use experts (brokers and attorneys) wisely.

CHAPTER FOUR

Merger Considerations

It bothers people when we tell them there are few true mergers between accounting firms. Perhaps mergers have some romantic image in people's minds. Or perhaps it's the misconception that mergers seem to be less risky, less individual, less work, and more of a "we're in this together" joint cause to make the new firm a success. In most cases, when people refer to merging accounting practices, one of the practices actually acquires the other and controls the newly formed firm. A true merger only takes place when neither practice acquires the other.

Why Are There So Few True Accounting Practice Mergers?

As complicated as they may seem, sales of accounting and tax practices are simple and clean compared to true mergers. In an acquisition model, Practice A buys Practice B. With the transfer of an appropriate level of capital, Practice A gains ownership and control over most or all of Practice B's core assets—staff, clients, equipment, etc. In the transition period, Practice B's owner and/ or partners will still be involved; but, in time, the owner and/or partners of Practice A will operate autonomously from their influence, making for a clear and defined transaction. This does not mean that the partners of the selling firm never become partners in the buying firm. They can, and sometimes the synergy is there to facilitate this term of sale.

In a merger model, negotiations are not transaction oriented, but rather focus on aligning the two practices with the idea of a long-term working relationship between the owners or partners of Practice A and Practice B. To be successful, the merged practices need to shed their individual identities and become a new practice—Practice C. They must develop an entirely new philosophy of practice and culture. This can be challenging, particularly for owners or partners who are change resistant or have tied their egos into the pre-merger business. Without the commitment to Practice C, the merger will flounder as each of the merged firms struggles to hold to its previous identity. The lack of commitment to Practice C will invariably lead to the development of an "us vs. them" mentality coupled with an "our accounts and their accounts" practice perspective.

A second reason there are few successful true accounting mergers is that in accounting and tax firms, as in any service company, people are the core product. This heightened value of you, your partners, and your staff makes mergers far more challenging than they are for product companies. Products don't have egos, feelings, roles, responsibilities, salary concerns, or benefit packages. Products are not required to adhere to specific policies or procedures.

For example, merging two practices may result in redundant functions—overstaffing in some service areas, under-staffing in other service areas, too many partners or senior partners, too high a payroll, or other issues related to staffing and personnel assignments. Therefore, redefinition and reassignment of roles and responsibilities is a critical step to complete prior to merging. Otherwise, key partners and employees may leave the merged practice and undermine its success.

Finally, successful true mergers of accounting firms are rare because the parties are either merging for the wrong reasons or are ill-prepared to merge. The merging parties often view the merger with rosy optimism and do not spend enough time planning effectively or addressing their doubts. It is all too common that a firm will seek a merger to resolve internal strife—lack of organization, poor management, or partner disagreements. Sadly, mergers rarely resolve these issues; instead, these issues typically infect the merged organization and lead to its failure and possibly dissolution of the merger. In general, bad mergers are driven by internal forces, like those mentioned above; while good mergers are driven by external forces—client needs, economic factors, or industry trends.

Contemplating a Merger

Before you decide to pursue a merger, it is important to examine your reasons for seeking a merger. As mentioned previously, there is good rationale for a merger that will lead to success, and there is poor rationale that may contribute to failure. It is critical that all owners and partners sit down, brainstorm, and discuss the reasons for a possible merger and their sequence of priority.

Good Reasons to Merge

Good reasons to seek a merger focus on facilitating the growth of the practice in a variety of areas including improving internal energy and opportunities for staff, adding new services and capabilities, and expanding the demographic or geographic reach of the business. Some examples of specific rationale that falls into each of these areas are:

Internal

- To increase key personnel to survive the loss or retirement of partners and valuable members of the firm

- To provide more promotional opportunities to staff

- To bring proven talent and fresh ideas into the mix

Service/Capabilities

- To pace growth of your clients and serve their increasing needs

- To better serve clients with new services by expanding staff and adding new expertise

Demographic/Geographic

- To gain exposure to larger and more diverse clients

- To expand into new locations where the firm doesn't have a presence

- To serve clients with branch operations in different locations

Reasons to Avoid a Merger

Poor rationale for seeking a merger tends to revolve around psychological resistance or individual partner needs. Here are some reasons to pass on a merger opportunity:

- You're happy and comfortable with the current size and functions of your practice.

- You are uncomfortable with the degree to which partner roles and responsibilities may shift—roles and authority of senior partners will be diminished or younger partners will be demoted.

- There will be a dramatic shift in style and method of interaction with clients.

- The merger will reduce or eliminate the perception of opportunities for advancement, which may result in the departure of the most productive staff members and those with the highest potential.

- There is limited commitment to the time needed to make the merger work.

- The partners are not comfortable with each other, the other firm, or the other firm's clients.

Preparing for a Merger

Finding a Merger Candidate

The process of finding a good merger candidate is similar to the process for finding a practice to acquire. Use the same avenues of contact—brokers, networking through professional organizations and referrals, advertising in industry periodicals, and listing on the Internet. In evaluating possible merger candidates, your criteria may differ from an acquisition because of the anticipated long-term relationship between owners and partners.

Turning Two Practices into One

Pre-merger planning is a bit more extensive than in an acquisition. You still need to do your homework and conduct more thorough due diligence, but you also need to conduct critical thinking and planning sessions with the merger candidate to ensure the merger will be a success. From first contact, it is essential that a clear, accurate analysis of each practice's position is provided and the reasons for seeking a merger as well as anticipated benefits of a merger are communicated.

The idea of turning two practices into one was mentioned earlier in this chapter with the example of Practice A and Practice B merging to form Practice C. For a "true" merger to be successful, it is critical that both practices shed their former identities and come together as a single team in the merged practice. There are a number of steps in facilitating this alignment. It is easiest if the merging companies can clear their heads, think of the merged entity as a completely new organization, and redefine all aspects of the business, including:

Marketing and Sales

- **Name**—Agreeing on the name of the merged firm can be an amazingly sticky point in the negotiation process. The earlier it is addressed, the easier it will be to resolve.

- **Brand**—Define how the logo, corporate colors, and marketing message are going to be presented to clients and the public at large.

- **Marketing Channels**—Determine which avenues the merged firm will use to approach the market: direct mail, advertising, referral partners, telesales, Internet, etc.

- **Affiliations**—Decide which association and organization memberships the merged firm should add, maintain, or drop.

- **Business Development**—Develop a process to turn prospects into clients and to expand existing clients into new services.

Internal Operations

- **Management Structure**—Unifying two management groups requires a new organization chart and, often, some significant shift in responsibilities.

- **Time and Billing**—Establish billing rates for all employees, develop forms for reporting billable hours, and provide instruction for reporting hours and expenses. Also, define how to differentiate billable hours from non-billable hours.

- **Personnel Policies**—These must be uniform for all full-time employees. This area may include insurance coverage, office hours, vacation, holiday and sick days, mileage reimbursement, stock options, and retirement accounts, among other things.

- **Quality Control**—Standardize all of the routine daily work from filing and paper management to handling phone calls—for example, define what is an acceptable time frame for returning a call.

Financial Operations

- **Budgets**—Budgets are a common area of divergence. Consensus on how much money will be allocated to each significant expense area is an important step in supporting the transition and achieving targeted goals.

- **Collection Process**—Establish client payment terms, billing cycles, allowable outstanding balance periods and amounts (if any), and collection procedures.

- **Debt Structure and Investment Policy**—Define firm parameters for acquiring a new credit line or accessing an existing one, as well as acceptable investment risks and the parameters for entering into an investment opportunity.

Steps to Negotiating a Merger

1. **Choose a strong negotiator.** If there are multiple partners in your firm, you should get together and select a single negotiator, because group negotiations typically fail. Keep in mind that the managing partner may be a good administrator but not necessarily the best negotiator. A negotiator with a history of diplomacy and tact is vital, since a successful merger will require close working relationships with the partners from the other firm.

2. **Exchange basic information.** Look beyond the financial statements and billing rates and include information along the lines of firm philosophies, personnel files, firm histories, organizational charts, and marketing plans. If each firm is up-front and open about sharing information regarding its finances, operations, and culture, the process of evaluating the likelihood of a successful merger will be less time consuming and more accurate.

3. **Forecast the profit and loss statements (P&Ls) and balance sheets.** First combine the P&Ls and balance sheets and eliminate any redundancy. Then make any additions or reductions based on the proposed operation of the merged firm. Be sure to account for a long transition stage and forecast several years into the future to identify profitability and growth milestones. Be honest and diligent. Lack of an acceptable profitability time frame should be a deal breaker.

4. **Thoroughly discuss core business structure.** This was covered in the previous section, "Turning Two Practices into One," but it is so critical that it needs to be reiterated. Be sure to thoroughly discuss each firm's existing marketing and sales initiatives, internal operations, and

financial operations. Then define how these elements will continue or change in the merged firm.

5. **Structure your partnership or ownership agreement.** Be certain to use an attorney well versed in business combination issues to assist in this step. This could make or break the deal. In general, your partner or ownership agreement should identify the managing partner, define partner roles and responsibilities, determine partner income levels, define partner investment and shares, and determine how retirement will be handled.

Pitfalls Unique to Merging

A merger, similar to a transactional exchange, has areas of heightened sensitivity that can undermine the success of the merged firm and, if unresolvable, perhaps lead to the dissolution of the merger. Being aware of these common pitfalls before entering into negotiations will help you better evaluate the potential success of a merger opportunity.

Lack of Profitability

Do not enter into a merger unless you can project profitability within a year or two.

Problems at the Partner Level

A merger is not a way to resolve partner conflicts. These are typically philosophical differences in nature, which a merger will not change.

Management Is Weak or Nonexistent

A merger results in a new firm perhaps twice the size of the merging firms. In a true merger, where neither practice acquires the other, someone must step forward and take control or chaos will prevail!

Cultural Differences Between the Firms

Often, so much time is spent looking at the positive reasons for merging that the firms don't really get to truly know each other's processes, cultures, or working procedures.

Overlooking the Post-Merger Challenges

Aligning processes, restructuring policies, and integrating personnel takes a tremendous amount of time, if done correctly.

Failure to Consider Weaknesses and the Potential Downside

How many baskets does the other firm have? Are all their eggs in one? If a key employee, client, or referral source decides to leave or retire, what happens to the firm?

Acting Too Quickly

A merger is a complicated process that takes time. If a firm is in a hurry to merge, it usually means something is wrong. Proceed with caution.

Failure to Involve People

The development of an "us" versus "them" mentality is natural after a merger. Combat this by mixing assignments and staff to integrate members of the two merger firms. You may even want to consider joint staff retreats or team-building exercises to facilitate the mixing process.

Discrepancies in Compensation of Partner and Staff

Pay is always a touchy subject. When merging two pay scales, be aware of any disproportionate areas and be prepared to adjust them.

MERGER CHECKLIST

Philosophy/Compatibility	Yes	No
In regard to both firms:		
● Are the firms' cultures compatible?	❏	❏
● Are the work ethics similar?	❏	❏
● Are the attitudes toward clients positive?	❏	❏
● Are the attitudes toward employees positive?	❏	❏
● Is the relationship between owners productive and beneficial?	❏	❏
In regard to the other firm:		
● Is it quality controlled oriented?	❏	❏
● Is it overly aggressive?	❏	❏
● Is it not aggressive enough?	❏	❏
● Are the types of clients the other firm has compatible with yours?	❏	❏
● Is it financially stable?	❏	❏
● Does it have a good reputation?	❏	❏
● Is there a probability of a hidden agenda on the other firm's behalf (e.g., personnel layoffs after the merger is consummated)?	❏	❏
● Do the partners want to be hands on?	❏	❏
● Do the partners want to play a large role?	❏	❏
● Do the partners want to be administrators?	❏	❏
● Do the partners want to be marketers?	❏	❏
● Do they want to take on a heavy workload?	❏	❏
● Do they want to take a smaller role?	❏	❏
● Is there a lot of overtime (billed or unbilled) on jobs?	❏	❏
● Are the profiles of the other firm's clients encouraging?	❏	❏
● Do they pay the firm on time?	❏	❏

MERGER CHECKLIST

History	Yes	No
● Is the other firm's claims and litigation history assuring?	❏	❏
● Are the results of the most recent peer review affirmative?	❏	❏
● Does the other firm have frequent mergers/splits?	❏	❏
● Are the mergers/splits too frequent?	❏	❏
● Has the other firm had a license or certificate suspended or revoked?	❏	❏
● Has it ever faced disciplinary action by a state or federal regulator (e.g., board of accountancy, NASD, SEC, PCAOB), a state CPA society, the AICPA, or other organization?	❏	❏
● Does the firm carry insurance? Type: _____	❏	❏
● Have you considered obtaining a background investigation report on the key partner (and telling them you are doing so)?	❏	❏

Scope	Yes	No
● Is the firm's work compatible with yours?	❏	❏
● Does its work complement yours?	❏	❏
● Will you be working collectively?	❏	❏
● Does the firm specialize in a certain area of practice?	❏	❏
● Are you familiar with that area of practice?	❏	❏
● Is their practice area more hazardous than yours?	❏	❏
● Are the rewards worth the risks associated with the deal if it falls apart?	❏	❏

MERGER CHECKLIST

Insurance Ramifications	Yes	No
● Have you considered the ramifications of your options carefully?	❏	❏
● Have you obtained an endorsement for Extended Reporting Period Coverage (ERPC), also known as "tail" coverage, which covers past work performed up until the date of a merger or dissolution?	❏	❏
● Have you found out:		
Whether "tail" coverage is available to you?	❏	❏
The period of time the ERPC covers?	❏	❏
The cost for the ERPC?	❏	❏
The coverage limit under the current policy and ERPC?	❏	❏
Who has consent to settle claims for prior work?	❏	❏
Whether there are differences in prior acts dates?	❏	❏
What insured limits and deductible the new firm will carry?	❏	❏
How the deductible will be divided?	❏	❏
Who will pay the premiums and/or deductibles?	❏	❏

Final Thoughts on Mergers

In this chapter, we took a brief look at the various aspects unique to true accounting practice mergers. In the initial section, we strove to emphasize the difference between a "true merger" and the common misuse of the term "merger" to describe a transaction that is actually an acquisition. With this understanding in mind, we looked at the stages of contemplating, preparing, and negotiating a merger. Also, since mergers are different from acquisitions, we included a section on pitfalls and a checklist specific to mergers.

It is true that lessons from this chapter, particularly the section on turning two practices into one, can be utilized and contribute great value in an acquisition process. It is natural and necessary, whether you are merging or acquiring, to take a fresh look at your internal processes, your financial structure, and your marketing initiatives. This type of self-examination can only strengthen those elements you already have in place.

If we can reinforce this chapter with a single final thought, it is to proceed with caution. Successful true mergers involve long-term working relationships, collaborative decision making, and strong management for the foreseeable future. Get to know the merger candidate like you know your own firm. Collaborate and determine how the firms are going to merge prior to finalizing anything. Most importantly, navigate the tricky steps of merging at a slow and comfortable pace.

CHAPTER FIVE

Financing an Acquisition

Many buyers strive to acquire a practice for as little cash down as possible. Buyers should realize that "no cash down" does not automatically mean that the seller will receive no cash at closing. The seller's cash down payment can come from outside financing. This chapter covers many of the facets of financing the practice acquisition, with a focus on utilizing an outside lender.

Frequent Questions on Financing

Thinking about leveraging an acquisition? Below are some questions frequently asked about financing:

- Is a down payment required to secure loan approval? How much?
- Why won't/can't the seller finance 100 percent of the purchase price?
- Will I need to use my home as collateral for financing purposes?
- How do I finance an employee/management buyout?

- Why is a good credit rating important?
- What are interest rates on practice acquisition loans?
- What are the terms on acquisition loans?
- My practice is for sale—should financing for buyers be a consideration?
- Can a seller note with a previous owner be refinanced?
- What is the success rate for practice acquisition loan approval?
- How long will it take for my loan to be approved? Funded?
- What are the elements necessary for a loan package and what do lending sources look for in reviewing an application?
- What is the optimal way to structure a deal for financing approval?
- What financing amounts are available for an acquisition?
- Do prepayment penalties exist?
- Are all SBA Loan Programs the same?
- Why is cash flow or adjusted net income important in a loan decision?
- How do revenue trends in the practice affect the loan outcome?
- Does the acquisition require additional assets for loan collateral?
- How are practices that include real property financed?

How Are Deals Financed?

Down Payment from Personal Funds, Seller Financed

A fairly common method of financing practice acquisitions is to use a combination of personal funds and seller financing. Personal funds are used for a down payment of 20–35 percent, and the balance is paid to the seller over some period of time with interest. The main hurdle is that the buyer needs to have significant liquid assets. For example, for a $300,000 practice the buyer would need a minimum of $100,000 in cash.

All Cash—Personal Funds or Financed

A buyer paying all cash for the acquisition is ideal, but few buyers are willing and able to do this. It does occasionally happen in the case of a buyer who previously sold another business, worked for a company and received stock options, or received an inheritance. However, most buyers who have accumulated the wealth required to purchase or finance an all-cash deal are probably looking at other investment opportunities. All cash may also require the seller to reduce the price since the risk of transition is placed entirely on the buyer.

Even when using borrowed funds, the lender would still require either: a) the buyer to inject 10–20 percent; or b) the seller to hold a similar amount as seller financing.

Banks and Finance Companies

Utilizing banks or finance companies is a good method of structuring the terms for acquisition. It allows the seller to exit without feeling the need to watch over the buyer's shoulder because he or she is concerned about being paid.

The choices are to obtain a loan backed by the Small Business Administration (SBA) or to use a conventional loan. Each has advantages and disadvantages.

Options for the financing of small business acquisitions have increased in recent years. More practices now qualify for SBA financing because there are flexible and intelligent lenders who understand the importance of cash flow. Even in a struggling economy, banks report increased lending to small businesses.

A Note on Deal Structures and Valuation

There are three basic structures for purchasing accounting and tax practices.

Earn-outs

During an earn-out, a buyer agrees to pay the seller a certain percentage of the billings over a certain period of time. For example, a buyer agrees to pay 25 percent for five years. Some might conclude this total equals 125 percent of gross. This is not necessarily the case. The buyer argues that the seller will receive more money because of increased fees over time and expanded services, etc. Why would a buyer want to pay more money than necessary? The only logical reason is for the increased security provided by a five-year guarantee. In fact, under some of these arrangements a buyer could change his mind with no additional liability.

Not all earn-outs are inappropriate, particularly when an earn-out is used as a portion of the final transaction value. For instance, an earn-out may be appropriate for an internal buy-sell by partners or for practices located in rural communities. However, we have found that the simpler the structure, the better the transaction's likelihood of success for all parties.

Fixed Price

This is an easy method of structuring a sale. The buyer agrees to pay a fixed price, and the terms can be anywhere from all cash at closing to a 100 percent installment note. Few practices are sold this way, but maybe more should be. Nearly all other types of businesses are sold using this method. It may necessitate lowering sales prices, but most sellers would readily discount for a simple structure.

This approach also eliminates some of the difficulties of the transition period. Frequently, a seller worries that a buyer is not doing all that is required to successfully retain clients. In such cases, the seller may feel the need to control the client contact. However, a buyer must be free to establish solid client relationships.

Even the best transition plan will not retain 100 percent of the client base. Our observations suggest that some clients will see the transition as a time to make a change and select a new CPA. Plan for some client reduction regardless of your expertise, and you will encounter fewer surprises.

Multiple of Annual Gross Billings

Currently, this is the most common structure we utilize. The buyer and the seller agree to some multiple of annual gross billings, usually at some point between 100–150 percent of the annual gross. The annual period can be historical or for a future period. This method only makes sense with a future period; otherwise, a fixed price structure should be used. With a future period, there will be some process identified for how to calculate the "billing guarantee" and how an adjustment is made. The documents in the appendix illustrate this process.

While other structures or hybrid structures exist, most transactions utilize one of these three methods.

See the "Valuation" section in chapter 3, *Selling Your Practice*, for more information on valuation methods.

Our Philosophy About Financing

We believe the best deals are where the buyer has some risk but not necessarily a huge cash risk or all of the risk. In other words, the buyer puts in some cash (10 percent), the buyer borrows a significant portion from a lender (60–80 percent), and the seller carries a promissory note for the balance (10–30 percent). This is advantageous to the buyer, because it moves the seller out of the practice a little sooner. The relationship with the seller is tricky— "too little" is bad and "too much" is bad. Think about learning to drive with your parents. Once you learned to drive, it was not much fun to drive with them. Having both the buyer and the seller in the practice long-term frequently leads to problems.

Another consideration is that banks can pool similar loans to reduce risk. A seller is probably going to sell one business and, therefore, cannot reduce the risk of carrying all-seller financing.

Financing Considerations for the Buyer

- Most practices are sold with at least 20 percent of the purchase price financed by the seller, who remains involved for a brief period to ensure a smooth transition. This amount may or may not be adjusted to account for estimated client retention.

- Your needs for operating cash will continue after the down payment is made and the transition is completed.

- Vigilant evaluation of your working capital requirements is vital. The last thing you want to do is make poor decisions due to inadequate working capital.

- Consideration of the funds required to maintain and grow the practice should be included in determining financing requirements.

- Creditors have the ability to kill your credit or to begin bankruptcy and/or foreclosure proceedings if payments are missed.

- Remember that not all banks are equal. Whether seeking a conventional or SBA loan, look for a lending institution with experience in accounting and tax practice acquisitions. Many loan officers over-promote their company's ability to provide suitable financing in an effort to win your business. Banks with expertise in this industry segment are sensitive to the capital requirements necessary for an acquisition.

Steps to Financing Your Acquisition

1. **Find a business.** After you have established your acquisition criteria, utilize existing resources to explore the market and find businesses of interest. This is covered in more detail in *The Buying Process* in chapter 2.

2. **Establish the purchase agreement or the deal structure.** The purchase agreement is typically created after an extensive process of interaction and investigation between the seller and buyer. When you reach this point in the process, be sure to create a thoroughly detailed purchase agreement. This is covered in detail in *The Buying Process* in chapter 2.

3. **Find and interview lenders.** There are many lending sources available. Carefully consider the size, type, and processes of each lender, and be sure they fit your needs and meet your goals. A list of possible lenders can be found in the resource section at www.prohorizons.com.

4. **Prepare required documents.** This can be a time-consuming process of gathering and creating documentation required by your lender. Grit your teeth and get it done so the process can move forward. A breakdown of contents of a typical loan application package can be found in this chapter under the section titled "Preparing Required Documents."

5. **Begin due diligence process.** Due diligence is a critical process to finalizing your loan. Like you, your lender will want to be sure that every rock has been turned over, examined, and looked under before the deal is finalized. More information on due diligence can be found in the "Due Diligence" section of chapter 2, and a complete checklist can be found in appendix C.

6. **Wait for the loan approval.** This step can take three to eight weeks. Clearly, there are quite a few variables. The loan approval process examines your history and the "5 Cs of Credit." More information regarding the loan approval process and the timing variables can be found in this chapter under the sections titled "Loan Approval" and "Timing."

7. **Assemble final loan and closing documents.** After everything has been examined, resolved, and any required changes have been made to the paperwork, you need to carefully assemble and verify your loan and closing documents.

Lending Sources and Issues

There are many factors to consider such as:

Size and Niche of Lender

Some smaller banks and commercial lending institutions may be more open and friendly to business credit. In these types of organizations, there may be one person who oversees all loan applications. Carefully choose the bank and officer who processes your business loan application. If providing a business plan, make sure that the loan officer has the experience to understand and interpret your presentation.

Larger commercial lending institutions typically have several officers to process business credit applications and can offer more choices and options.

Specialty lenders are commercial lending institutions that focus on specific types of business financing, such as financing for professional practices.

The Loan Officer

Potential practice owners often treat loan officers like an adversary, as if the parties are butting heads over the loan approval. On the contrary, the loan officer wants to provide the loan and build a business relationship. To approve a loan, the lender must understand:

- The intended use for the funds

- The applicant's track record and operational experience

- Terms and feasibility for repayment

As a reminder, use your rapport-building skills to learn about the lender's process, staff, and policies. Evaluate the officer's ability to establish a relationship and educate you about each step of the process. While every officer brings his or her own individual experience and risk tolerance to the process, there are ways you can build an advocacy relationship that may lead to a more rewarding experience.

> **Do I need to provide collateral for financing to buy a business in most instances?** Yes. If you have collateral, the financial institution will most likely accept it! However, not having collateral doesn't necessarily mean you won't get financing as long as other factors look good—the cash flow in the deal, your credit history, and your background experience. All factors are considered. All lenders will want at least a first position lien on the business being acquired, and many will want a secondary source of collateral or repayment, usually your personal residence. Additionally, if you already own a practice, the lender will want a lien on that as well; most likely over time the businesses will blend, and they will be unable to distinguish one from the other.

The loan officer's process often follows these steps:

1. Understand your motivation and collect loan information.

2. Determine your credit rating.

3. Issue a letter of interest.

4. Submit to loan committee.

5. Relay results.

Preparing Required Documents

While the process can be time consuming, frustrating, and intimidating, being informed and prepared will improve your chances of securing the desired capital for your acquisition.

Many lenders require the following information in the loan application package:

Financial Documents

- Personal Financial Statement
- Buyer's Income Tax Returns (personal and business for last three years)
- Seller's Income Tax Returns (business for last three years)
- Current (Interim) Income Statement and Balance Sheet
- Cash Flow Projection based on actual historical data

Application Documents

- Buyer's Résumé
- Purchase and Sale Agreement (or Letter of Intent)
- Equipment list including estimated values
- Articles of Incorporation/Partnership Agreement/LLC Agreement, if applicable

- Lease Agreement (for commercial property only)
- Assignment of Lease (for commercial property only)
- Lessor's consent to Assignment of Lease
- Franchise Agreement, if applicable
- Insurance Information, after loan approval

SBA Documents

- Owner/Seller's IRS form 4506 Verification from Tax Returns
- SBA Form 4 Application for Business Loan
- SBA Form 912 Statement of Personal History
- Photocopy of Resident Alien Status Visa, if applicable
- Loan Request Statement
- Business history and description
- Seller's Statement of Reason
- Verification of Cash Injection and Source
- Cash flow projections

In compiling a comprehensive loan package address the questions below:

- What is the specific purpose of the loan?
- What amount of financing is required?
- When are funds required and for what period?
- How will sufficient cash flow be generated for loan repayment?
- What collateral can be utilized, if applicable?
- Will a personal guarantee be provided?

Critical Factors

Lending decisions are mostly based on mathematics: Are debt-to-equity and debt service-to-cash flow ratios in line? Find out what criteria your lender is examining. If the lender is looking at these ratios and yours are in line, and you have a strong credit rating, the likelihood of loan approval is reasonable.

Loan package presentation matters. Lending decisions are made by human beings; so, neatness, presentation, and prompt responses are important. If you present a sloppy package, it turns off the reviewer. In addition, lending decisions are often made by a committee, which receives the loan officer's recommendation along with your loan package. An influential officer who feels confident about advocating on your behalf is certainly beneficial.

Your receptiveness to feedback and suggestions regarding structure, information, collateral, and required guarantees strengthens your application. Rely on the loan officer's expertise regarding the institution's policies and procedures.

Loan Approval

After your package has been submitted, your loan officer puts together the case for your loan request. He or she assembles the documents for your application that may include information such as:

- Practice ownership
- Banking activity
- Previous borrowing experience
- Information from third-party credit reporting agencies

The lender analyzes your application based upon a combination of several factors, primarily the **"5 Cs of Credit"**:

- **Credit History**—Does the borrower have a history of paying required amounts?

- **Cash Flow (critical)**—Does your practice show evidence of the ability to repay the loan?

- **Capacity**—Is there a secondary source of repayment?

- **Character**—Does the borrower have high integrity?

- **Collateral**—What collateral can the borrower put up to secure the loan? This is not always necessary for cash flow loans but frequently required.

Timing

The amount of time required for a response varies by the lending institution and by the number of people involved:

- Loan officer decides to submit—two to five days

- Loan officer and manager decide—five to seven days

- Local loan committee or loan underwriter makes decision—one to two weeks

- Out-of-town committee decides, as in a larger regional or national bank—one to four weeks

So, you can expect the process of securing a loan to take three to eight weeks depending on the steps taken and the decision makers involved by your lender.

Final Thoughts on Financing

Financing the acquisition can be a complex process. It subjects both the buyer and the seller to examination and some inconvenience. We often hear things along the lines that the lender is asking for too much information and "nit-picking." These are natural feelings when you are unfamiliar with the details of financing. However, a thorough understanding of the needs of the lender and the process of securing a loan will make your experience more positive.

If we can leave you with a final thought from this chapter, it is to tackle the paperwork. Pursuing an acquisition can be challenging without the need of financing. The burden of paperwork needed to secure a loan can seem a bit overwhelming. Like most things in life, the anticipation is far worse than the reality. So, grit your teeth and dive into the process.

Keep in mind when the loan process has been successfully completed, several objectives will have been met:

- The seller has sold his business and has money in hand.

- The buyer has acquired the practice at fair terms.

- The bank has made an investment in the success of the borrower.

CHAPTER SIX

Life Cycle of a Sale

So far, we have covered the buyer experience, the seller experience, the valuation process, financing, and due diligence. All are helpful in setting the foundation of the sales process; however, only passing reference has been made to the direct interaction between the buyer and seller. What actions or reactions are expected of the seller, and what are the corresponding actions or reactions of the buyer? What happens when? What is the time frame? What is done individually, and what is done mutually?

The life cycle of the sale may vary from transaction to transaction, but there are standard stages and steps that are consistent in all acquisitions. In this chapter, we will present a comprehensive sale timeline defining the sequence of events for the seller and the corresponding sequence of events for the buyer. Then, we will break down the timeline and summarize each milestone as it occurs.

The graphic on the following page represents the usual stages in a complete sale life cycle.

The Life Cycle of a Sale Timeline

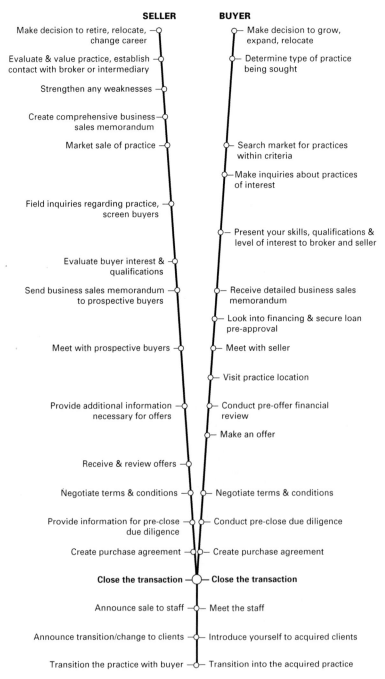

SELLER   **BUYER**

Make decision to retire, relocate, —○   ○— Make decision to grow,
change career   expand, relocate

Evaluate & value practice, establish —○   ○— Determine type of practice
contact with broker or intermediary   being sought

Strengthen any weaknesses —○

Create comprehensive business—○
sales memorandum

Market sale of practice —○   ○— Search market for practices
                                        within criteria

                                    ○—Make inquiries about practices
                                        of interest

Field inquiries regarding practice, —○
screen buyers

                                    ○— Present your skills, qualifications &
                                        level of interest to broker and seller

Evaluate buyer interest & —○
qualifications

Send business sales memorandum —○   ○— Receive detailed business sales
to prospective buyers   memorandum

                                    ○— Look into financing & secure loan
                                        pre-approval

Meet with prospective buyers —○   ○— Meet with seller

                                    ○— Visit practice location

Provide additional information —○   ○— Conduct pre-offer financial
necessary for offers   review

                                    ○— Make an offer

Receive & review offers —○

Negotiate terms & conditions —○   ○— Negotiate terms & conditions

Provide information for pre-close —○   ○— Conduct pre-close due diligence
due diligence

Create purchase agreement —○○— Create purchase agreement

Close the transaction —○— Close the transaction

Announce sale to staff —○— Meet the staff

Announce transition/change to clients —○— Introduce yourself to acquired clients

Transition the practice with buyer —○— Transition into the acquired practice

© 2005 Professional Horizons Inc.

Independent Action Milestones

Seller

Make the Decision to Retire, Relocate, or Change Careers

As we've discussed, the idea of selling your practice is usually the result of one of these personal decisions. These decisions may be driven by age, wealth, environment, health, or some other personal life factor. In essence, you have a chain of events and thoughts leading to your decision to sell. For example, too much work leads to too much stress, which leads to a desire to change careers, which leads to the decision to sell your practice.

Evaluate and Value Your Practice, Establish a Relationship with a Broker or Intermediary, and Strengthen any Weaknesses

This is the process of sizing up your practice. Where are you strong and where are you weak—services, staff, clients, revenue, expenses, cash flow, etc.? At this point, it is wise to establish a relationship with a broker or intermediary. This will provide you with a fresh, objective set of eyes for evaluating your practice as well as the expertise of knowing where to look and what to look for. A specialized accounting firm broker is knowledgeable about the market and the factors that motivate buyers to buy. Through the evaluation process, you will compile the data needed to determine the practice value. In addition, analysis of the practice weaknesses may provide some quick fixes that will strengthen the practice and increase the value.

Buyer

Make the Decision to Grow, Expand, or Relocate

The idea of buying a practice is usually the result of professional decisions, although personal life factors usually come into play. On the professional side, you may be looking to grow by adding talented staff, adding new services, acquiring competition, acquiring new clients, and expanding into new territory; or you may be simply beginning or building your first practice. On the personal side, you may be looking to relocate in order to change your environment or reduce your cost of living. Similar to the seller's motivation, it is a chain of events and thoughts that lead to the decision to buy—slow business development leads to increased need of new clients, which leads to the idea of acquiring new clients, which leads to the decision to buy an existing practice.

Determine Type of Practice Being Sought

The decision to buy a practice may dictate some of the criteria of the practice being sought—location, staff in place, services offered. Size of the practice is important to determine both in regard to cash flow or earning potential and in regard to number of clients. Finding the right balance between positive growth and overwhelming workload is important. Also, taking some introspective measures of your skills in regard to management, technology, interpersonal interaction, and business development will help you build criteria that fit your capabilities.

Seller

Create a Comprehensive Business Sales Memorandum

The business sales memorandum is the first significant point of information sharing between the seller and the buyer. It should be well structured, professional, and detail all of the core aspects of your business. In essence, it should contain all of the information needed for a buyer to take the first step toward acquisition.

Market Sale of Your Practice

Go find your pool of buyers by networking, advertising, direct mailing, and/or listing with a broker. Be sure to promote your sale to a geographically and demographically diverse group of practice owners. Also, be careful to maintain as much confidentiality as possible.

Buyer

Search Market for Practices with Criteria and Make Inquiries About Practices of Interest

With your criteria established, you can begin to search the market for practices of interest. To start with, check local or state association newsletters, industry periodicals, local newspapers, and brokerage Web site listings. When you find a practice of interest, make an immediate inquiry, get answers to your initial questions, and verify how serious the seller is about selling.

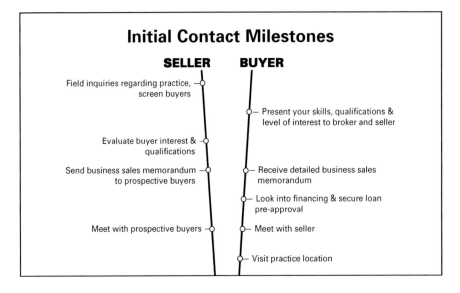

Initial Contact Milestones

Seller

Field Inquiries Regarding Your Practice and Screen Buyers
To streamline the process and time frame, it is important to have a plan in place regarding inquiries. Be sure to do more than just gather contact information. Use the first call and every subsequent contact as an opportunity to gauge the buyer's interest and capability.

Buyer

Present Your Skills, Qualifications, and Level of Interest
Provided both parties are interested, there will be follow-up conversations after your initial inquiry. It is important to use these opportunities for more than information gathering. Be sure to present yourself, your capabilities, and your interest when appropriate. The seller will be weighing much more than finances in choosing a buyer.

Seller

Evaluate Buyer Interest and Qualifications and Send Business Sales Memorandum

Based on your initial screening and the prospective buyers' presentations of their skills and interest, you will be able to isolate your serious prospects and take the next step toward closing the sale. Before sending the business sales memorandum, be sure the prospective buyer has received, signed, and returned a confidentiality agreement.

Buyer

Receive Business Sales Memorandum and Look into Financing

The business sales memorandum provides you with your first look into the details of the practice for sale. Use this document as an initial measure of the fit with your purchase criteria and goals. If the practice is still appealing, you should begin to put the mechanisms of acquisition in motion by setting up a meeting with the seller and possibly looking into any loan or financing assistance you may need.

Seller

Meet with Prospective Buyers

This is the first significant opportunity to size up your prospective buyers and take a significant step toward closing the sale. The buyer will arrive with many questions. Be sure to answer them, but don't forget to ask your own questions. Your goal is to determine whether you, your staff, and your clients can work with the prospective buyer and whether you are comfortable with the buyer's level of enthusiasm, technical competence, and professional qualifications.

Buyer

Meet with Seller and Visit Practice Location

This is the buyer's opportunity to make a strong first impression and further investigate details of the business. An enthusiastic, high-energy presentation of your experience and interest will go a long way to winning over the seller. Also, be sure to investigate the seller's motivations and background as well as conduct a surface level examination of the professionalism of the practice and the staff.

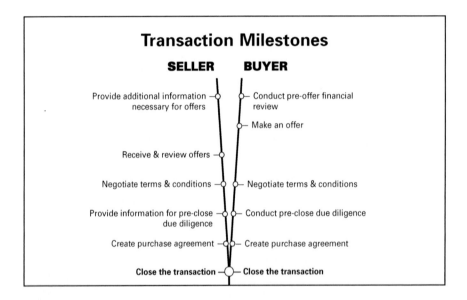

Transaction Milestones

Seller

Provide Additional Information Necessary for Offers

Provided the meetings with a prospective buyer went well, the buyer should express interest in making an offer and may request additional information to assist in the formation of an offer. Information requested may include basic financials, a copy of your practice valuation, an estimate of annual client loss rate, and details regarding top account activity and trends. Be sure to protect critical proprietary information, such as your client list, at this stage and to avoid giving a buyer a "test drive" of your business.

Buyer

Conduct Pre-Offer Financial Review and Make an Offer

In requesting information from the seller for your pre-offer review, be sure to examine just the level of information you require to form a comfortable offer. Trying to uncover too much too early may make the buyer question your motives and sour the deal. Once you have examined any requested information and are satisfied by the findings, a letter of intent to acquire the practice should be drafted and sent to the seller. At a minimum, the letter of intent should detail purchase price and terms, a non-competition agreement, the length and details of a transition period, and a targeted closing date.

Seller

Receive and Review Offers

Style and content of letters of intent to acquire a practice can vary greatly. At first glance, an offer may appear to be lacking in some areas but should be carefully reviewed as it may contain some attractive terms. When reviewing offers, determine whether the down payment and terms are sufficient and whether the prospective buyer has strong credit scores. Also, keep in mind which prospects have the best skills and ability to continue the success of the practice.

Seller and Buyer

Negotiate Terms and Conditions

The seller usually initiates negotiation of terms and conditions by sending a counteroffer in response to the letter of intent. Both parties need to be careful about how they conduct negotiations. Having a solid understanding of the transaction process, the negotiable elements, and your role will help to smooth any bumps in this stage of the transaction.

Seller

Provide Information for Pre-Close Due Diligence

This is a much more in-depth follow-up to the pre-offer financial review. It is not usually necessary but the buyer may bring in outside advisors to help with the review. Be helpful and cooperative throughout the process or the buyer may feel you are hiding issues. With that said, also guard the names of clients and other proprietary information that is not directly relevant to the sale of the practice.

Buyer

Conduct Pre-Close Due Diligence

Remember that "caveat emptor" applies as in all business transactions; so, be sure you perform a thorough investigation prior to closing the sale. Keep in mind that there is no such thing as too much due diligence. The specific review materials needed vary and are up to your discretion. It can be a time-consuming process, but it is important that you make it as intricate and involved as you require.

Seller and Buyer

Create the Purchase Agreement and Close the Transaction

When the buyer has completed the due diligence process and is satisfied with all aspects of the business, he or she will prepare the purchase agreement and other closing documents for review and approval by all parties. At this point, the deal is still fragile, so proceed cautiously. Renegotiating any points previously agreed upon can kill the deal. In addition to the purchase agreement, the buyer should sign the promissory note, the bill of sale, and transfer the necessary funds (check or wire) to close the sale.

Transition Milestones

SELLER **BUYER**

Announce sale to staff ─○─ Meet the staff

Announce transition/change to clients ─○─ Introduce yourself to acquired clients

Transition the practice with buyer ─○─ Transition into the acquired practice

Transition Milestones

Seller

Announce the Sale to Staff and Announce the Transition/Change to Clients

Avoid any sudden shifts or changes after closing the transaction. This eliminates additional stresses while employees and clients adjust to the change and become acquainted with the buyer. As soon as the transaction is closed, the seller should hold a meeting to announce the sale to the staff. This should quickly be followed by a "meet the new owner" gathering to give the staff a scheduled opportunity to meet the buyer.

Buyer

Meet the Staff and Introduce Yourself to the Acquired Clients

Like the staff, clients should be notified as soon as possible regarding the sale of the practice. A mix of phone calls, mailings, and meetings should be used to announce the sale and introduce the buyer. A strong focus should be put on pledging a continuation of the quality services provided, in addition to introducing any new services, capabilities, or announcements.

Seller and Buyer

Transition the Practice

With the announcements and introductions to staff and clients taken care of, it will be important to notify vendors and business partners and align the organization under the buyer's management. This may require redefinition of personnel assignments, policies, and processes, as well as the seller's training the buyer in the existing client structure and service offering. In addition, the seller typically remains supportive and available for reasonable short-term consultation.

Final Thoughts on the Sales Life Cycle

As you can see, there is a good deal of back and forth interaction between the seller and buyer in our sales model. It is really only during the independent action milestones that the two are working autonomously of one another. Once the initial contact is made, it becomes a process of corresponding actions and reactions.

You might find yourself in a transaction where almost all of these milestones apply, or you might discover some of them are not relevant. Our final thought on this chapter is—whether you are selling or acquiring, be sure to take your time, respect the other party's needs and responsibilities, and adjust and utilize the applicable milestones mentioned to make your sales or acquisition process a success.

CHAPTER SEVEN

Land Mines, Pitfalls and Issues to Avoid

Buying or selling an accounting or tax practice is a dynamic process requiring constant attention to details and extensive decision making. If you make the right decisions and choices, the purchase will be a success, and you are on your way. If you make poor decisions and choices, you can ruin your career and your financial well-being.

In this chapter, we'll look at the most common and most detrimental mistakes made when buying or selling an accounting or tax practice.

Selling Your Practice for Too Little

This usually occurs when the seller does not receive professional advice regarding the initial sales process, the seller uses simple rules of thumb, or the buyer and seller conduct their own negotiations.

Surely you have heard the old adage that accounting and tax practices sell for one times gross revenue. Blanket rules of thumb are far from the whole story. Compare two firms both grossing $350,000. Firm A has high fees with a net of $200,000. Firm B has lower fees, and the profit is only $135,000. Simplistic valuation assumptions would have each owner believe his practice is worth $350,000. Practices differ, and as with any business, the ultimate valuation is based upon many tangible and intangible factors that go well beyond the gross revenue.

Without understanding this concept, the seller may overlook key points to support the asking price for the practice. Combine this with conducting direct negotiations, and the seller can find himself or herself at an unfair disadvantage.

For example, let's say the seller and buyer hit it off. As a result, the seller loses objectivity, while the buyer dominates the conversations by subtly pointing out gaps and limitations in the seller's practice. The seller considers the accuracy of these claims and weighs them against how well he or she likes the buyer and how strong a fit the buyer would have with existing clients.

The buyer may have valid points of concern, but a seller with an experienced advisor could diminish the importance and impact

---

On a Personal Note

In our editorial review, there was some debate regarding our repeated reference to enlisting the services of a broker to avoid several of the following pitfalls. I think one of the great faults of humanity is believing that we can do it all ourselves. When we fail to avail ourselves of expert guidance, we risk getting it wrong. The number one reason we do this is to save some money. What if I told you one of the reasons I'm a broker is that I believe a good broker saves his clients time, money, and legal hassle by facilitating successful transactions? So, I recommend hiring and working with a broker as a way to avoid several of the pitfalls in this chapter. This chapter is perhaps the most critical element of this book and for me to not mention this recommendation would undermine the value and service this book is striving to provide.

of any objections. Also, the comfort between seller and buyer should be an important consideration, maybe the most important consideration, but it needs to be kept in perspective and separated from the price and terms negotiations.

Low Price Example

A couple of years ago a CPA called our office to inquire about selling his practice. We talked several times, and he decided, since he was in a major metropolitan area with a strong market, to run an ad and sell the practice himself. He conducted a "for sale by owner."

A few months later, a buyer we were working with on another practice called to tell us he decided to purchase the practice of a CPA he met on his own. It turned out it was the same CPA who called our office several months earlier. The buyer's rationale was that he could acquire a "for sale by owner" practice for much less money. He used the same lender we introduced him to and knew he had a really good deal.

As it turned out, the buyer did acquire the practice for the old rule of thumb of 1.0 times gross—for a purchase price of approximately $650,000. The same practice would easily have sold for 1.25 times gross based upon its high profitability and our assessment of the current market. This seller and buyer resorted to the one times gross revenue rule, and the seller sold his practice for $160,000 less than its value.

Avoid Selling for Too Little

First, have a thorough understanding of the value of your practice. This provides defensible rationale for the price you set. Then, hire a consultant or business broker who specializes in the sale of accounting firms. In addition to bringing a wealth of knowledge and experience to the process, the broker will work as your intermediary.

It is critical that you meet with the buyer and evaluate his or her skills, work ethic, and personality. Having a broker at hand to provide perspective and handle your negotiations will help you stay objective and separate the closing price from any personal connection you may have with the buyer.

Wasting Time on Unqualified Buyers

Even if you discount the time, effort, and cost of finding prospective buyers on your own, the process of qualifying buyers can sink the sales process.

First, there is the time spent on casual inquiries. These may include competitors comparing their practice to yours, or may be accountants who fantasize about buying the perfect practice under the perfect circumstances if they had the means; so, they inquire to see if you own the dream practice. They are not serious about buying but will waste your time if you let them. We are talking about a significant amount of your time as you will find most of your inquiries fall into this category.

Then, there are the somewhat serious buyers who are not willing to pay a fair price, cannot get financing, or do not have the skills and ability to continue the success of your practice. Unfortunately, it takes time and effort to uncover these limitations.

Finally, you have a small pool of buyers who are ready, willing, and able to pay a fair price and settle on fair terms and who will serve your existing clients well. These are the prospects worth your time.

Avoid Wasting Your Time on Unqualified Buyers

Consultants, advisors, brokers, and financing partners should have established procedures, forms, and checklists to quickly qualify buyers. In some cases, they will even have a list of existing well-qualified buyers in your area. Let them do the leg work so you can focus your conversations on the three to six serious buyers who can make the sale a success for you, for themselves, and for your clients.

Selling to the Wrong Buyer

This is closely tied to the previous pitfall. When we say "wrong" buyer, we are referring to the buyer who does not have the ability, the required skill set, or the desire to provide sufficient service to your existing client base. As the seller, finding the "right" buyer should be a large part of your focus, particularly if you are settling on contingencies in your sales agreement. Defining the "right" buyer depends on your practice and your unique circumstances. See chapter 3, *Selling Your Practice*, for information about defining the "right" buyer.

Promoting the sale of your practice, finding and qualifying buyers, and thinning the prospective buyer pool can be a time-consuming and tiring process. By the time you settle on a final pool of serious prospects, you will likely be worn out and want the process to come to an end. As a result, you may not have the appropriate perspective or conduct enough follow-through to identify and differentiate the "wrong" buyer(s) from the "right" buyer(s).

Avoid Selling to the Wrong Buyer

Let an intermediary do the up-front, dirty work of generating, qualifying, and thinning out the prospective buyer pool. This will allow you to conserve your energy and time so you can focus your efforts on identifying the "right" buyer.

Settling on Unsatisfactory Terms or Contingencies

Terms and contingencies are typically structured with the intent of relieving the buyer of the burden of full payment. In addition, the intent is to award the seller more money over a specified period of time in return for the flexibility.

The challenge lies in the fact that once the sale is closed, the entire burden of fulfilling any terms or contingencies falls on the buyer. In other words, the seller has little or no influence over the impact of the contingencies. Many sellers structure client retention clauses expecting to receive 1.25 to 1.5 times their gross revenue and end up receiving less than 1 times their gross. This hurts the buyer, too, as it means that the anticipated growth and return on investment from the acquired clients has not been realized.

What we really mean is that earn-outs put an inappropriate burden on the seller. (See the "Structure of Transactions" section in chapter 3, *Selling Your Practice*, for more information on earn-outs.) The seller may guarantee the first-year revenue, an excellent

Buyer Is Too Busy with His Current Practice

A CPA we will call Sam Seller sold his practice to Bruce Buyer, a fellow CPA he knew from his local chapter. Sam was eager to move out of state. Bruce had been in practice for many years and had a loyal client base. Sam's practice was not far from Bruce's. Sam felt that Bruce provided quality services to his clients.

So, they worked out a purchase arrangement that would pay Sam 25 percent of fees Bruce collected on Sam's clients for five years. Sam wished he had received some money up-front, but he was happy he was able to work out a deal that would pay him 125 percent of his annual billings; plus he saved broker and attorney fees.

What Sam did not realize was that Bruce was extremely busy, especially during tax season. Bruce figured he could do most of Sam's work himself and the rest could be done by his secretary or new junior accountant. They were unable to properly serve all of Sam's clients, and, of course, Bruce's loyalty was to his longtime clients. Sam's clients began to drift away and find other accountants to do their work. To complicate matters, Bruce did not like some of Sam's clients, and he asked them to find a new CPA. In short, the deal fell apart. A majority of Sam's clients had left by the end of the second year.

As a result, Sam may end up receiving only 30–50 percent of what he expected.

"win-win" strategy, but should not need to guarantee the buyer's complete success. The seller's job is to get the clients in the door, the buyer's job is to keep the clients and identify additional services to meet the clients' needs.

Avoid Unsatisfactory Terms or Contingencies

Both parties need to conduct thorough due diligence. If revenue guarantees are part of the settlement, is the buyer going to be successful in meeting the expectations? Is the seller's practice structure and client base going to help or hinder the buyer's effort to make the transition work?

These questions address a broad area of concern. In detail, they should question, among other things, the buyer's workload, work ethic, and commitment to assimilating and serving a large new client pool. On the flip side, the question examines whether the seller's clients are organized in a way to facilitate assimilation, how many clients the seller has, whether similar services are being offered, and how many work hours are required to maintain existing services.

By structuring contingencies that take a thorough understanding into account and that are achievable, you will create a "win-win" agreement.

Not Planning for Sufficient Client Loss

Client loss is going to be a factor in any sale of an accounting or tax practice. It is nearly unavoidable.

A client may leave for a variety of reasons. He may be relocating. He may have had an unfortunate first encounter with the buyer. Perhaps his three phone calls were not answered. Perhaps he hasn't been contacted by the buyer. Perhaps he was unhappy with the seller and saw the sale as an opportunity to break ranks. Perhaps he sold his business and is no longer in need of the same level of services. Whatever the reason, an average of 10–15 percent of existing billings is usually lost in the year following the sale of a practice.

Avoid Underestimating Client Loss

First, find out what the typical client turnover of the seller is and start from there. Some sellers retain nearly 100 percent year to year, others lose 15 percent per year. Next, adjust your revenue forecasts by projecting a significant loss of existing billings, say 20–25 percent. We are not saying that this will happen, but you want to avoid going into this situation with "rose-colored glasses." How does that impact your bottom line? Can your practice survive with these revised revenue estimates? If not, be sure you have a contingency plan that includes a cash reserve to support you in the worst case scenario.

With your contingency plan in place, do everything you can to retain the existing business—an introductory "welcome" mailing,

Examine the Trends of the Client Base to Estimate Loss

A lucrative practice was sold in San Francisco. What remained undiscovered by the buyer was that over the years, many clients had moved and continued to mail in their information for their taxes. The buyer also did not know that several clients were planning to retire and sell their businesses.

After a year, the buyer had lost 30 percent of the billings. When the buyer and seller began to examine the reasons, it was quickly discovered where the client loss was coming from—many of the mail-ins had stopped and two clients had sold their businesses. If the buyer and seller had seriously considered these in the initial price and billing guarantee, the actual adjustment would have been minimal and expected.

In the end, both the buyer and the seller agreed there was not much that the buyer could have done to increase the billings.

personal calls to top accounts, quick responses to any inquiries, etc.—while honing your business development skills. It sounds simplistic, but if you can build new business at a higher rate than your loss of acquired accounts, it will result in a net increase in revenue.

And finally, don't focus solely on individual accounts and become discouraged when you lose a few clients. It's going to happen. Instead focus on increasing the overall billings of the practice and adding new clients to the mix. Operate from an abundant market mentality.

Breaching Confidentiality

There is nothing that will undermine the sale of a business quicker than a breach in confidentiality. It destroys employee focus, productivity, and sense of security. It creates client uncertainty and amplifies the level of potential client loss. It provides competitors with the leverage they need to overcome your clients' loyalty and take accounts from your practice.

Avoid Breaching Confidentiality

Be sure you are dealing with professionals who understand the paramount importance of confidentiality. Do not assume this is understood automatically. The risk is similar for both the buyer and the seller, but outlining rules of confidentiality and having written confidentiality agreements are necessary steps at the beginning of the process. It is important to observe strict confidentiality regarding your pending transaction in all aspects of your life, including:

Family

Selling or buying a practice is a huge decision and, in most cases, will have a tremendous impact on your family. Discussing such a decision with your spouse, siblings, and/or parents may be an important part of the process for you. Be sure to include the need for confidentiality and the reasons behind that need with any family members included in the process. You would be amazed how often idle chitchat at the coffee shop, grocery store, hair salon, or dentist's or doctor's office has led to a severe breach in confidentiality.

Brokers or Intermediaries

There are two confidentiality benefits to working with a business broker or other intermediary to facilitate the sales process. First, since this is their profession, they will advocate strict confidentiality. If they know their business, they know that confidentiality is critical. If you have to advocate confidentiality to them, change to a broker who has a better understanding of its importance.

Second, because you are working with a broker or other intermediary, you can remain anonymous. A good broker will not provide detailed information about your practice until a potential buyer is qualified and has signed a confidentiality agreement. This ensures that the curious competitor, client, or employee uncovers nothing until you announce the sale. This wouldn't be true if your home or cell phone number was the primary contact number on the sales advertisement.

> **A Breach in Confidentiality**
>
> I had a CPA tell me a story recently of how one of his clients learned he was considering selling. In fact, he really had not gotten started on the sale of his practice; he was in the early stages of his decision. The seller had a nine-year-old son who told a playmate they would be moving out of state. The playmate told his father who happened to be a client. The client asked the CPA whether he was planning to move and sell his practice. He had to let the client know that nothing was imminent, but he would be the first to know. Sufficient to say, family is a frequent group where confidentiality is inadvertently breached.

Your Office

Interoffice communication is also a common source of a breach in confidentiality.

- Do you have a private fax and/or e-mail that no one else in the office can access? If not, you should either set one up or be sure the parties involved never send a message or fax regarding the sale of a practice.

- Does anyone else ever check your voice messages or your e-mail for you? If so, be sure you either change your passwords, or, again, be sure the parties involved do not leave or send messages regarding the sale.

- Do you have a direct line, or do your calls go through a receptionist? If your calls go through a receptionist, be sure parties involved with the sale remain ambiguous regarding the reason for their call. A cell phone is always a great alternative to the office lines.

- Do you have a locked filing cabinet, or are the files in your office accessible? If anyone gets curious, a stray file can let the cat out of the bag. Keep everything under lock and key until you are ready to announce the news.

Automatically Selling to an Employee or Partner

If you polled practice owners, many would probably agree that selling to an employee or partner is a preferable sales scenario. After all, you groom your successor as he or she gains hands-on, working knowledge of your practice and good relationships with your clients. Unfortunately, this seldom proves to be a positive sales experience.

First, there are the years spent grooming your successor so he or she can eventually take over the practice. This involves a significant investment in time and energy. In the end, there are no guarantees your time and effort will be rewarded with a viable successor. We have heard from many sellers how their trusted successor left the practice, taking with him or her the seller's succession plan.

Perhaps you are fortunate and you end up with a viable successor. If so, you will find you may need to relinquish some of the control over his or her time frame. This will be partly because of your sense of both your and your successor's values in the day-to-day operation of the practice and partly because of your desire to avoid disrupting critical day-to-day activities that generate cash flow. The sale will only take place when your successor is comfortable taking over, when the workload is accommodating, and when any needed financing and logistical issues can be ironed out.

Finally, because of your familiarity and comfort with this individual combined with his or her sense of value regarding the future of the practice, you will likely settle for less money than you should. Sales of this nature typically involve long-term buyouts, discounted sales prices, and unwanted contingencies.

Avoid Automatically Selling to an Employee or Partner

Don't automatically settle on an employee or partner as your buyer. This does not mean that you should never sell to an employee or partner; just avoid making him or her the only option. Instead, consider the employee or partner as one of your finalists in a pool that includes at least a few buyers from outside the business. This keeps you in control of the timeline, price, terms, and any contingencies in the final sales agreement. An employee or a partner who is serious about buying rather than having the practice handed to him or her will step up and compete with the other serious prospects. If the employee or partner does step up, you can give him or her preferential treatment at that time. If he or she does not step up, it will be clear that you should definitely sell to an outside buyer.

Focusing on One Buyer

This is similar to the previous pitfall. Even though you may have already decided to whom you will sell your practice when the time comes, we urge you to reconsider. Even if you are sure there is only one viable buyer in your area, don't make the mistake of limiting your options.

Having multiple buyers engage in the sale of your practice has many positive impacts. Top among these, it allows you to look for and evaluate the best fit, and it gives you greater flexibility in obtaining the price and terms you desire. In a best case scenario, you will end up with two great candidates who must have your practice. The result will probably be that you sell your practice for a higher price and under better terms than you had imagined.

Avoid Focusing on One Buyer

Conduct a broad marketing campaign to promote the sale of your practice. Be sure to include practice owners from your market area as well as the major urban areas in your state and possibly the surrounding states. Two of the major motivations for buying a practice are relocation and building a regional office presence to broaden your market reach.

If you choose to sell on your own, be forewarned. Depending on location, we usually receive ten to fifty serious candidates for the sale of a practice; so, you will need to be prepared to conduct some aggressive qualifying to thin out your prospective buyer pool depending on the breadth of your marketing campaign.

Waiting Too Long to Sell

There are two variations to this pitfall. First, waiting too long to sell—your practice is declining as annual revenue drops, there is much more competition in the area than there used to be, or the geographic layout of the area has changed making your location less desirable.

Then, there is taking too long to sell. In other words, letting the sales process drag on too long. Selling your practice is a major distraction that requires time and energy. This is time and energy spent away from providing services and generating billable hours. The resulting downward spiral as the sales process drags along is a steady decline in revenue, which will ironically result in a reduced sales price.

Avoid Waiting Too Long to Sell

In regard to waiting too long to sell, it is a good idea to start the process in advance of the time you plan to sell. This will provide you with several benchmark figures that contribute to the overall value of your practice. Keeping an eye on key indicators, such as location and competition, while working to ensure continued growth in your revenue stream will enable you to forecast an appropriate time to sell.

Avoid a drag in the sales process by bringing someone on board, such as a broker or professional intermediary, whose primary focus is selling the practice. Your involvement in key phases will still be required, but let your intermediary handle the day-to-day activity and the bulk of the work. The amount of distraction you are subject to will be greatly reduced and will allow you to work on maintaining or even increasing the revenue generated by your practice, resulting in an anticipated or higher than anticipated price when you close the sale.

Conducting Insufficient Due Diligence

As in any major purchase, an in-depth inspection is a vital part of the evaluation process prior to buying an accounting or tax practice. Due diligence is a process that examines the critical factors in the operation and management of an accounting practice as well as verifying representations made by the seller.

When due diligence is done haphazardly or incompletely, the

buyer is left vulnerable to unexpected and hidden issues. When a thorough due diligence is performed, those unexpected and hidden issues are revealed, taken into account, and adjusted for in price, terms, or contingencies. If truly catastrophic, the revealed issues would likely break the deal.

Avoid Conducting Insufficient Due Diligence

Some will say there is no such thing as too much due diligence. However, you want to avoid "analysis paralysis" and will, at some point, need to take a leap of faith to finalize the sale (see the "Due Diligence" section of chapter 2, *Acquiring a Firm*, for more information). The general rule of thumb is to trust but verify.

To facilitate this process, establish a detailed and thorough due diligence checklist. An appropriate checklist for your needs should be provided if you work with a professional sales consultant, or you can locate one on the Internet or in printed resources (there is a sample checklist in appendix C). Use the checklist to carefully examine the seller and the practice you might acquire. In addition, discuss experiences with other accountants who have bought practices and try to get an overview of their buying experience. They may provide insight beyond your checklist.

Finally, if you work with a broker, do not rely solely on him or her for the due diligence process. The broker may be of some help, but ultimately you, the buyer, are responsible for the thoroughness of the review.

Being a Lone Ranger

This is really the culmination of all the pitfalls mentioned earlier in this chapter. When you go it alone, you are relying on your own resources—experience, time, budget—and, even with this book in hand, there are going to be some tough lessons learned. All of the preceding examples are very common and very real experiences people have had when they sell their practices on their own.

Your goal should be to sell your practice to the best buyer you can find, for the most money you can receive, under the best terms possible, and with the least impact on your clients and your business operations. Unless you have the experience and processes in place this requires a monumental effort:

- Valuing your practice

- Packaging your practice

- Timing the sale

- Marketing your practice

- Identifying prospective buyers

- Qualifying prospective buyers

- Conducting negotiations

- Working through due diligence

- Settling on price

- Structuring terms and conditions

- Creating a purchase agreement

- Transitioning the business

Splitting Focus Can be Costly

A colleague of mine worked for a product company that spent so much time and focus on selling the business that it was distracted from the effort of marketing and selling its products. The potential buyer dragged out the due diligence cycle, and, since marketing and sales efforts were decreased, the company's revenue started to decline. Guess what? Eventually the declining revenue became apparent to the potential buyer, and he decided to pass on the acquisition. The result was a huge revenue slump that the company never did overcome. Five years later, the company sold for one-third of the price the seller had negotiated with the potential buyer who stepped away from the acquisition.

You need to work through all of this while maintaining business as usual. In addition to managing all the extra work, you need to figure out how to keep it all confidential, which is a real challenge when you are the key contact for inquiries.

Avoid Doing Everything Yourself

Working with an intermediary, advisor, or broker is not a necessity. You can sell on your own. However, hiring a broker who specializes in the sales of accounting and tax practices is the most effective path to closing the sale of your practice. Although you will still be responsible for a considerable amount of work, a good broker will handle the most challenging portions of the sales process and provide you with the structure needed to best utilize your time and streamline your involvement.

The growth of the brokerage industry over the past decade, coupled with the growth of the Internet, offers today's practice owner with a wide range of brokerage options. Following are some of the key questions you should ask when selecting a broker:

Is the broker doing the work?

Absentee brokers and e-brokers might make great claims, but be sure they are working for their fee. Some e-brokers are little more than matchmakers and only provide you with a Web listing that buyers visit—you deal directly with the buyer and manage the entire sales process. Finding a buyer is a valuable service but not worth 5–8 percent of your final sale price. This is particularly true when most full-service brokers will do everything for the same or a slightly higher percentage of the final sale price.

How does the broker market?

Look for a broker who conducts integrated marketing campaigns—combining e-mail, Web, mail, advertising, and telesales to contact buyers. This is a measure of professionalism—the broker isn't cutting corners—and ensures your sale is announced to a wide range of diverse prospects.

Does the broker specialize?

As in any industry, accounting and tax practices pose unique and specific issues during the sales process. Working with a broker who specializes in accounting and tax practice sales will ensure that all of the details are covered and no considerations are overlooked.

What is the broker's experience and background?

First, find out how many sales your broker has closed. In addition, has he ever owned and sold his own accounting practice? Having a broker who has been in your shoes can be a real asset when push comes to shove.

What data can the broker provide?

Is there any data a potential broker can provide that will give you peace of mind? This may include:

- Number of sales closed in the past twelve months and past six months
- Average number of inquiries for a sale listing
- Number of active buyers in his or her database
- Details of how he or she will market your practice:
  - Site listing coupled with site traffic data
  - Advertising
  - Mail pieces—when and how many?
  - Other initiatives—e-mail or phone
- Range of services the broker provides
- Average length of time the broker's listings are on the market

Can the broker back up his or her claims?

Brokering is a sales business. The first sale a broker must complete is convincing you to list with him or her. To do this, some brokers overreach their abilities or the market realities. A popular example of this is claiming that you will get 100 percent cash at closing with no contingencies. That would be nice. The reality is that few buyers are willing to take that risk. The result is that your practice is listed for an extensive period of time, potentially never sells, or you may be forced to reduce the asking price well below its value to close the sale. Brokers are aware of this and usually make this claim to get your business with the intent of later renegotiating with you.

Can you talk with past sellers?

Any credible broker is going to have past sales successes. Is he or she willing to let you talk with past sellers? This will give you a solid perspective into the workings of the broker's sales process and any of his or her strengths and weaknesses. Of course, these are going to be the broker's best clients, but that does not make their experiences any less valuable. Who knows? You could soon be one of the broker's best clients as well.

Final Thoughts on Land Mines, Pitfalls, and Issues to Avoid

Selling or acquiring a business can be a remarkably complex experience. For the seller, there may be a sizable amount of emotion tied to the business and the clients as well as a bit of uncertainty regarding the future. For the buyer, there may be some fear and caution about taking on the potential acquisition and the financial risk required.

It is challenging to stay objective, open, and professional when there is the perception of so much personal investment at stake. On top of the practice sale or acquisition, you need to maintain your existing business productivity. Understanding this, it is not surprising that we have presented eleven common issues to avoid.

Whatever course you choose to pursue, please keep these pitfalls in mind. They are real and all too common. Finally, avail yourself of any expert advice you can, whether it be in the form of an accountant who has sold his practice, a lawyer, a financial advisor, an intermediary, or a broker.

CHAPTER EIGHT

In Closing

Whether you decide to sell, acquire, or merge on your own or you decide to work through an intermediary, we hope that you have found answers to your questions within these pages. Involvement in any type of business transition can be challenging, to say the least. Hopefully, you now have enough of an understanding to successfully navigate the process.

There are many conclusions that can be drawn from the preceding pages. So, in our closing thoughts, we would like to isolate and summarize a few of the key messages this book has presented.

Set Your Goals and Make a Plan

Determine from the start why you would like to pursue a transaction. Be honest with yourself, your family, your partners, any advisors you utilize, and the other party involved in the transaction. If you are looking to sell and are tired of the business or are moving on to a new endeavor rather than planning to retire, your goals, time frame, and ability to offer transitional support may vary dramatically.

Define the goals you would like to achieve through the completion of the transaction. For the seller, these may include security for your clients, security for your staff, a specific amount of cash at closing to fund the next phase of your life, or ongoing involvement in the practice. For the buyer, these may include expanding your client base or regional coverage, adding experienced staff, or broadening the range of services you provide.

Consider the timing for closing the transaction. Tax season is a busy period in this industry and a difficult time of year to make a transition. Determine the ideal timing for you and the business. Then, expand it to a range of several months to account for unexpected bumps in the process. Set up your plan with enough lead time to work through and complete the process within that range of time.

With this foundation for a plan, you will be able to communicate your needs and goals clearly to the other party and, working together, be more likely to achieve a "win-win" agreement through the transaction process.

Understand the Process and Implement It

Knowledge of the landscape you are going to traverse is the most important aspect of getting to your destination. When traveling, it helps us prepare for everything from our modes of transportation and expenses to the attire we should wear and supplies we should bring. In a practice sale or acquisition, understanding the process and steps ahead will similarly help you prepare as you traverse unfamiliar and tricky territory.

Pursuing implementation of a process does not mean that everything will go according to plan. There will be bumps in the road, adjustments that need to be made, and some challenges to be met. However, with a process in hand, you will be better prepared to identify these issues for what they are, to deal with them, and to get the transaction back on course.

Do Not Become Overwhelmed and Bogged Down

Knowledge of the process and work ahead can have a negative impact as well. It can make the overall effort appear quite daunting. The result may be that the first step, and every step thereafter, is difficult to complete. Do not let the complete picture overwhelm your ability to undertake the individual steps and actions needed to move the transaction forward.

Also, be careful that you do not let yourself become stuck in an individual step. The initial steps, the due diligence phase, and the loan approval process are the most common areas where this seems to happen, but any step can become a challenge if neglected. Taking small measures and actions within each step will keep things moving forward, and before you know it, you will be one step closer to closing the transaction.

Maintain a Positive Outlook

Belief is a powerful force. I have seen the belief in the other party's goodwill and in the spirit of the agreement overcome some of the trickiest negotiations. I have also seen lack of those beliefs allow minor contingencies to undermine the close of a transaction. You can only establish a "win-win" agreement if each party feels like he or she "won." The elements needed to achieve this were presented in chapters 2 and 3 and are so important that we are going to reiterate them.

The key components in completing a successful business transaction are:

- Good rapport with all parties involved

- A mutual understanding of the terms of the agreement

- A mutual awareness of the roles and emotions of both the buyer and seller

- Belief that all parties are committed to a good transaction and a successful transfer

Beware the Many Pitfalls

Ignoring the potential pitfalls you could encounter in the transaction process is similar to driving while wearing a blindfold. The ability to swerve to avoid a mishap is only as good as your ability to see and anticipate a possible collision with that obstacle. If you are not aware of the possibility, there is little you will be able to do to avoid the issue. So, please take heed of the land mines, pitfalls, and issues we have detailed in the previous chapter.

Again, it is our hope that you will be able to take from this book the information you need to ensure that your practice sale or acquisition has a positive outcome. It can be a remarkably rewarding experience when it is approached and handled appropriately. Best of luck as you move forward with your process!

Additional Information

Following is an appendix with relevant sample forms, letters, resources, and contact information. The forms, letters, and selected other material from this book can also be downloaded from our Web site at www.prohorizons.com/resources/forms. Use your last name as the login, enter your e-mail address, and enter the following password **B4USBRT**.

Contacting the Author

John Ezell is happy to receive any of your questions or feedback regarding this book and to discuss any needs you have in regard to your sale or acquisition plans. He can be reached at 800-729-7034 or john@prohorizons.com.

Internet Resources

This appendix contains a listing of Internet resources you may find useful in your effort to sell or acquire an accounting practice. The resources include a few Web site listings for:

- Accounting and General Business Brokerage Firms
- Internet Accounting Resources and Tools
- Classified Advertising for the Accounting Industry
- National Associations for the Accounting Industry

Internet Resources

http://www.prohorizons.com
ProHorizons is a consulting and brokerage firm specializing in the buying, selling, merging, and building of accounting and tax practices.

http://www.bizbuysell.com
Inexpensive national business for sale Web site. Many businesses for sale but few CPA and EA firms.

http://webcpa.com
Tools and resources for the electronic accountant.

http://www.search.rja-ads.com/aicpa
The Journal of Accountancy classified advertisements.

http://www.natptax.com/classified_ads.html
The National Association of Tax Professionals classified advertisements.

http://www.naea.org
The National Association for Enrolled Agents Web site.

http://www.nsacct.org
National Society of Accountants Web site.

http://www.aicpa.org
The American Institute of Certified Public Accountants Web site.

http://www.accountantsworld.com
The Web site of the Community of Independent Accountants.

http://www.cpaclassifieds.com
E-mailed weekly with a circulation that exceeds 180,000 accounting professionals.

http://www.cpanet.com
An online community and complete resource for the accounting profession.

It is also important that you review the state societies' and associations' Web sites. Many of them are an excellent resource in starting your search.

Sample Documents

This appendix contains several sample documents you may find useful in your effort to sell or acquire an accounting practice. The resources include:

- A Sample Letter of Intent to Acquire
- A Sample Letter for a Seller Announcing the Sale to Clients
- A Sample Letter for a Buyer Introducing Himself or Herself to Clients
- A Sample Confidentiality Agreement

Sample Letter of Intent

BUYER'S LETTERHEAD
<Date>

<Seller>
<Seller's Address>
<Seller's City, State, Zip>

Dear <Seller>:

This letter will serve as a **Letter of Intent** on behalf of
_____ to acquire from you the accounts to which
you are presently providing accounting services and the goodwill
associated therewith.

The following expresses our understanding with respect to the matters
described herein, but is expressly understood that this **Letter of Intent**
does not constitute a complete statement of, or a legally binding or
enforceable agreement or a commitment upon me or you with respects
to matters described herein:

1. Purchase Price
Buyer will pay a multiple of ___ times the annual gross billings of the
firm based on the first year of operations, estimated at _____, plus
$_____ for the furniture and fixtures, and under the following terms:

$_____ as a deposit to be held by ProHorizons and paid to you
at closing and credited toward the purchase price.

$_____ as a down payment to be paid at closing and to be
credited toward the total purchase price.

$_____ to be financed by you, the Seller, for _____ (__) years
at __% rate of interest with payment terms as follows: monthly
payments of $_____ beginning _____ (__) days after the
closing.

2. Non-Competition Agreement

The Seller will execute a non-competition agreement that will exclude the Seller from soliciting or servicing the accounts being sold to me for ___ years.

3. Transition Period

The Seller will agree to assist the Buyer in an orderly transfer of the firm for ___ (__) days immediately following the closing, not to exceed _____ (__) hours. Seller will make himself available (by phone, fax, etc.) to answer questions regarding client issues and introductions during the Transition Period at no charge. *The Seller agrees to be available during the period _____ to _____ for additional transitioning and the Buyer agrees to compensate the Seller for such time at the rate of $_____ per hour.*

4. Closing

My attorney will draft all the necessary contracts and closing documents to be presented to you for your review prior to closing. The closing date will be no later than _____ at a time and location to be agreed upon later.

5. Miscellaneous

Other items such as the use of names, phone numbers, collection of receivables, employment contracts, broker fees, the proration of prepaid expenses and taxes, and anything else not addressed above will be discussed and agreed to prior to closing.

Upon mutual signing of this **Letter of Intent**, I will authorize my attorney at my expense to draft all the appropriate documents.

This **Letter of Intent** is subject to the satisfactory verification of the Seller's records by the Buyer.

_____
<Proposed Purchaser>

_____
<Seller>

Sample Letter: Seller Announcing Sale to Clients

SELLER'S LETTERHEAD
<Date>

John D. Client
1234 Main St.
Metro City, CA 12345

Dear Mr. Client:

It is with both excitement and regret that I write this letter to you, for my relationship with my clients has grown beyond the professional level, and you have been friends to me. However, I have decided to retire this year and will no longer be able to provide your tax and accounting needs.

I have been looking for someone with high professional standards to take over my practice. I wanted someone who is highly personable, whose tax and accounting abilities are topnotch, and whose office is in the same area so you are not inconvenienced. I have found those qualities in <Buyer>.

<Buyer> has been in practice locally for _____ years. <Buyer> is well-qualified and you will have continuity of representation in all your tax matters. Since I will be transferring your files to <Buyer>, we have agreed to stay in contact should there be any questions about your situation. <Buyer> will be taking over my practice on <date>.

I am confident that your tax and accounting needs will continue to be well-taken care of and that the high-quality service in which I have invested so much time will continue.

I thank you for past business and friendship. Best wishes to you.

Sincerely,

<Seller>

Sample Letter: Buyer Introduction to Clients

BUYER/SELLER LETTERHEAD
<Date—A week to ten days after closing>

John D. Client
1234 Main St.
Metro City, CA 12345

Dear Mr. Client:

I have been asked by <Seller> to take over your tax and accounting needs. I just wanted to write you to introduce myself, to welcome you, and to let you know how pleased I am for this opportunity to be of service to you.

<Seller>, as you might expect, is concerned that the transition is smooth and with little or no inconvenience to you. To accomplish this, <Seller> and I have taken the following steps:

1) Made arrangements to transfer your tax records to my office, where they will be readily available so that I can assist you in case of government inquiry, loan verification, tax consultation, etc.

2) Assigned you a preferential, prescheduled appointment before my calendar begins to fill. You, of course, may change the appointment if it is not convenient. We have attempted to make it as close as possible to last year's appointment.

3) (Seller) will be available to this office for any questions that may arise concerning your past returns, in case of government inquiry or audit.

4) I will make myself available, either by phone or by appointment, to meet with you prior to your tax appointment so we can get to know each other in advance. Should you need year-end planning, as many do, especially with the new tax law changes, I will be happy to schedule an appointment for you.

We want the transition to be pleasant and comfortable for you. If there is anything you need or something I can help you with, please call. We are here to help.

I have reviewed <Seller's> fee schedule and found it to be essentially the same as our firm's, so unless there is some special circumstance, you can expect the fees to remain the same.

I have placed you on my newsletter mailing list and your first issue will arrive <date>. I look forward to meeting you in the near future.

Sincerely,

<Buyer>

Sample Confidentiality Agreement

CONFIDENTIALITY AGREEMENT and acknowledgment between

_____ (the Seller) and

_____ (the Buyer)

Recognizing that the transaction to purchase or sell an accounting practice naturally involves receipt of detailed information and that even disclosure of certain information could cause damage to these parties, the Buyer and Seller agree to protect each other's confidentiality. The parties promise not to disclose or to discuss with any third party that the accounting practice may be for sale, exchange, merger, or transfer.

The Buyer and Seller further agree not to disclose any facts learned about each other's businesses or Buyer's financial position to any third party, including employees, customers, clients, or other prospective buyers. Information and/or records obtained shall not be used for competitive purposes in any business, present or future.

At the conclusion of our discussions, and upon demand by the Buyer or Seller, all information, including written notes, photographs, memoranda, or notes taken shall be returned to the Buyer or Seller. This information shall not be disclosed to any employee or third party unless they agree to execute and be bound by the terms of this agreement.

It is understood that the undersigned shall have no obligation with respect to any information known by the undersigned or generally known within the industry prior to the date of this agreement, or which becomes common knowledge within the industry thereafter.

_____

Prospective Buyer   _Date_

_____

Prospective Seller   _Date_

Due Diligence Checklist

This appendix contains a sample due diligence checklist that may be useful in your effort to sell or acquire an accounting practice. This sample checklist should, at most, be considered a starting point in your effort to create a comprehensive due diligence checklist. Some areas have been left blank to encourage you to analyze and evaluate the needs and concerns unique to your pending transaction.

Due Diligence Checklist

Many potential buyers confuse a comprehensive due diligence review with obtaining the information necessary to evaluate whether the practice is a good acquisition. We believe the two should be separated.

Every buyer should first evaluate the potential acquisition using criteria developed in chapter 2, *Acquiring a Firm*. There are no perfect practices, so be sure your criteria are not too restrictive.

It is only after the seller has been met, the practice has been reviewed, and an offer has been made and accepted that the buyer should develop comprehensive due diligence information and a review checklist, such as the one below to search for areas of concern.

To start with, obtain and review the following information:

Financial Information

✔ Three years of tax returns

✔ Three years of financial statements

✔ Comparative year-to-date financial statements, current year compared to previous year with explanation of key variances

✔ Monthly profit and loss statement for current year

✔ Copies of monthly bank statements for the past two years

✔ Accounts receivable aging

✔ List of all physical assets included in the sale

✔ Monthly statements for any loan/line of credit accounts

✔ Detail of all insurance-related expenses for past two years

✔ Copies of insurance policies and loss history

✔ Detail of all computer software and related expenses for past two years

✔ Detail of tax-related expenses for past two years

✔ Detail of other significant expenses for past two years

✔ List and amounts of all owner discretionary expenses for past two years

✔ Summary and amount of all out-of-area clients

Contracts and Commitments

✔ Copy of facility lease agreement

✔ Copies of any other contracts/obligations of the company, including equipment leases

Personnel

✔ List of employees with title, years of service, copies of personnel files, and salary

✔ Copy of personnel-related policies (including employee manual, recruiting, evaluations, etc.)

✔ Copy of any compensation/benefit plans provided to employees

✔ List of any employee disputes or legal issues

Other

✔ List of all computer and other IT systems currently used in the company

✔ Copy of all marketing materials

✔ Criteria used to determine if a new client should be taken on and to determine if an existing client should be kept

✔ Copy of billing policy and procedures

✔ Copy of credit and collections policy

✔ List of any IRS preparer penalties

✔ List of any late tax payments made by the firm

✔ List of any legal issues or disputes with IRS

✔ Brief description of the history of the company

Provided nothing has developed that caused great alarm (i.e., IRS preparer penalties beyond what was expected), it is now time to move toward your due diligence analysis. Remember you are not performing an audit of the financial statements. You are performing analysis to ensure that you enter into this transaction knowing your risk. Similar to creating an audit program, each buyer should develop his or her own due diligence review checklist. Below is a starting point for addressing some of the potential areas of concern.

Sample Due Diligence Analysis

Review the current year financial statement for variances with the prior years:

- Is revenue growing or being maintained?
- Are all negative expense variances explainable?
- Have total expenses declined or grown only in relation to revenue growth?
- _____
- _____
- _____
- _____

Review the profit and loss statements

- Do expenses appear reasonable relative to your experience in practice?
- _____
- _____
- _____

Review bank statements

- After adjusting for line of credit withdrawals, is total cash deposited equal to cash basis revenue?

- Are bank fees and expenses normal (i.e., no large number of NSF charges)?

- _____

- _____

- _____

- _____

Review A/R aging

- Are most accounts relatively current (i.e., under ninety days)?

- _____

- _____

- _____

- _____

Prepare a cash flow analysis using the profit and loss statements and adjusting them for your personal cash requirements (i.e., debt service, modified personnel)

- Do you have adequate cash flow to meet your expenses?

- After removing 25 percent of your revenue and adjusting your personnel costs, are you still able to meet the debt service and make your minimum income requirements?

- _____

Review a sample of client files

- Does the work performed compare reasonably to the amount billed?

- _____

- _____

- _____

Other steps as necessary

State Boards of Accountancy

Following is a listing of all of the state boards of accountancy. The state boards are a useful resource for information regarding current licensing requirements as well as for verification of a license held by any potential buyer or seller of a practice.

State Boards of Accountancy

Alabama State Board of Public Accountancy
P.O. Box 300375
Montgomery, AL 36130-0375
Phone: 334-242-5700
Fax: 334-242-2711
Web: www.asbpa.state.al.us

Alaska State Board of Public Accountancy
Dept. of Community and Economic Development
Division of Occupational Licensing
Box 110806
Juneau, AK 99811-0806
Phone: 907-465-3811
Fax: 907-465-2974
Web: www.dced.state.ak.us/occ/pcpa.htm

Arizona State Board of Accountancy
100 N. 15th Avenue, Room 165
Phoenix, AZ 85007
Phone: 602-364-0900
Fax: 602-364-0903
Web: www.accountancy.state.az.us/

Arkansas State Board of Public Accountancy
101 E. Capitol, Suite 430
Little Rock, AR 72201
Phone: 501-682-1520
Fax: 501-682-5538
Web: www.state.ar.us/asbpa

California Board of Accountancy
2000 Evergreen Street, Suite 250
Sacramento, CA 95815-3832
Phone: 916-263-3680
Fax: 916-263-3675
Web: www.dca.ca.gov/cba

Colorado State Board of Accountancy
1560 Broadway, Suite 1340
Denver, CO 80202
Phone: 303-894-7800
Fax: 303-894-7802
Web: www.dora.state.co.us/accountants

Connecticut State Board of Accountancy
Secretary of the State
30 Trinity Street
P.O. Box 150470
Hartford, CT 06115
Phone: 860-509-6179
Fax: 860-509-6247
Web: www.sots.state.ct.us/SBOA/SBOAindex.html

Delaware State Board of Accountancy
Cannon Building, Suite 203
861 Silver Lake Boulevard
Dover, DE 19904
Phone: 302-744-4500
Fax: 302-739-2711
Web: www.professionallicensing.state.de.us

District of Columbia Board of Accountancy
941 N. Capitol Street NE, Room 7200
Washington, DC 20002
Phone: 202-442-4461
Fax: 202-442-4528
Web: dcra.dc.gov/information/build_pla/occupational/accountancy/
    index.shtm

Florida Board of Accountancy
240 NW 76 Drive, Suite A
Gainesville, FL 32607
Phone: 850-487-1395
Fax: 352-333-2508
Web: www.myflorida.com

Georgia State Board of Accountancy
237 Coliseum Drive
Macon, GA 31217-3858
Phone: 478-207-1400
Fax: 478-207-1410
Web: www.sos.state.ga.us/plb/accountancy/

Guam Board of Accountancy
Suite 508, GCIC Building
414 W. Soledad Avenue
Hagatna, GU 96910-5014
Phone: 671-477-1050
Fax: 671-477-1045
E-mail: guamcpa@ite.net
Web: www.guam.net/gov/gba/

Hawaii Board of Public Accountancy
Dept. of Commerce & Consumer Affairs
P.O. Box 3469 335
Merchant Street (96813)
Honolulu, HI 96801-3469
Phone: 808-586-2696
Fax: 808-586-2689
E-mail: accountancy@dcca.hawaii.gov
Web: www.hawaii.gov/dcca/pvl/areas_accountancy.htm

Idaho State Board of Accountancy
P.O. Box 83720
Boise, ID 83720-0002
Phone: 208-334-2490
Fax: 208-334-2615
E-mail: isba@boa.state.id.us
Web: www.state.id.us/boa

Illinois Board of Examiners
505 E. Green, Room 216
Champaign, IL 61820-5723
Phone: 217-333-1565
Fax: 217-333-3126
E-mail: boe@advancenet.net
Web: www.illinois-cpa-exam.com

Illinois Public Accountants Registration Committee
Public Accountancy Section
320 W. Washington Street, 3rd Floor
Springfield, IL 62786
Phone: 217-785-0800
Fax: 217-782-7645
Web: www.dpr.state.il.us

Indiana Board of Accountancy
Indiana Professional Licensing Agency
Indiana Governmental Center South
302 West Washington Street, Room E034
Indianapolis, IN 46204-2246
Phone: 317-232-5987
Fax: 317-232-2312
Web: www.state.in.us/pla/bandc/accountancy/

Iowa Accountancy Examining Board
1920 S.E. Hulsizer Avenue
Ankeny, IA 50021-3961
Phone: 515-281-4126
Fax: 515-281-7411
Web: www.state.ia.us/iacc

Kansas Board of Accountancy
Landon State Office Building
900 S.W. Jackson, Suite 556
Topeka, KS 66612-1239
Phone: 785-296-2162
Fax: 785-291-3501
Web: www.ksboa.org

Kentucky State Board of Accountancy
332 W. Broadway, Suite 310
Louisville, KY 40202-2115
Phone: 502-595-3037
Fax: 502-595-4281
Web: cpa.state.ky.us

State Board of CPAs of Louisiana
601 Poydras Street, Suite 1770
New Orleans, LA 70139
Phone: 504-566-1244
Fax: 504-566-1252
Web: www.cpaboard.state.la.us

Maine Board of Accountancy
Dept. of Professional & Financial Regulation
Office of Licensing & Regulation
35 State House Station
Augusta, ME 04333
Phone: 207-624-8603
Fax: 207-624-8637
Web: www.maineprofessionalreg.org

Maryland State Board of Public Accountancy
500 N. Calvert Street, 3rd Floor
Baltimore, MD 21202-3651
Phone: 410-230-6322
Fax: 410-333-6314
Web: www.dllr.state.md.us/license/occprof/account.html

Massachusetts Board of Public Accountancy
239 Causeway Street, Suite 450
Boston, MA 02114
Phone: 617-727-1806
Fax: 617-727-0139
Web: www.state.ma.us/reg/boards/pa

Michigan Board of Accountancy
Dept. of Consumer & Industry Services
P.O. Box 30018
Lansing, MI 48909-7518
Phone: 517-241-9249
Fax: 517-241-9280
Web: www.michigan.gov/cis/0,1607,7-154-10557_12992_
    13878—,00.html

Minnesota State Board of Accountancy
85 E. 7th Place, Suite 125
St. Paul, MN 55101
Phone: 651-296-7938
Fax: 651-282-2644
Web: www.boa.state.mn.us

Mississippi State Board of Public Accountancy
5 Old River Place, Suite 104
Jackson, MS 39202-3449
Phone: 601-354-7320
Fax: 601-354-7290
E-mail: email@msbpa.state.ms.us
Web: www.msbpa.state.ms.us

Missouri State Board of Accountancy
P.O. Box 613
Jefferson City, MO 65102
Phone: 573-751-0012
Fax: 573-751-0890
Web: www.ecodev.state.mo.us/pr/account/

Montana State Board of Public Accountants
301 S. Park
P.O. Box 200513
Helena, MT 59620-0513
Phone: 406-841-2389
Fax: 406-841-2309
Web: www.discoveringmontana.com/dli/pac

Nebraska State Board of Public Accountancy
P.O. Box 94725
Lincoln, NE 68509-4725
Phone: 402-471-3595
Fax: 402-471-4484
Web: www.nol.org/home/BPA

Nevada State Board of Accountancy
1325 Airmotive Way, Suite 220
Reno, NV 89502
Phone: 775-786-0231
Fax: 775-786-0234
Web: www.cpa@nvaccountancy.com

New Hampshire Board of Accountancy
6 Chenell Drive, Suite 220
Concord, NH 03301
Phone: 603-271-3286
Fax: 603-271-8702
Web: www.state.nh.us/accountancy

New Jersey State Board of Accountancy
124 Halsey Street, 6th Floor
P.O. Box 45000
Newark, NJ 07101
Phone: 973-504-6380
Fax: 973-648-2855
Web: www.state.nj.us/lps/ca/nonmed.htm

New Mexico Public Accountancy Board
111 Lomas Boulevard, Suite 510
Albuquerque, NM 87102
Phone: 505-841-9108
Fax: 505-841-9101
Web: www.rld.state.nm.us/b&c/accountancy/index.htm

New York State Board for Public Accountancy
State Education Department
Division of Professional Licensing Services
89 Washington Avenue
2nd Floor East Mezzanine
Albany, NY 12234-1000
Phone: 518-474-3817 ext. 160
Fax: 518-474-6375
Web: www.op.nysed.gov/cpa.htm

North Carolina State Board of CPA Examiners
1101 Oberlin Road, Suite 104
P.O. Box 12827
Raleigh, NC 27605-2827
Phone: 919-733-4222
Fax: 919-733-4209
Web: www.state.nc.us/cpabd

North Dakota State Board of Accountancy
2701 S. Columbia Road
Grand Forks, ND 58201-6029
Phone: 800-532-5904
Fax: 701-775-7430
E-mail: ndsba@state.nd.us
Web: www.state.nd.us/ndsba

Accountancy Board of Ohio
77 S. High Street, 18th Floor
Columbus, OH 43215-6128
Phone: 614-466-4135
Fax: 614-466-2628
Web: www.acc.ohio.gov/

Oklahoma Accountancy Board
4545 Lincoln Boulevard, Suite 165
Oklahoma City, OK 73105-3413
Phone: 405-521-2397
Fax: 405-521-3118
Web: www.oab.state.ok.us

Oregon State Board of Accountancy
3218 Pringle Road SE, #110
Salem, OR 97302-6307
Phone: 503-378-4181
Fax: 503-378-3575
Web: www.boahost.com/index.lasso

Pennsylvania State Board of Accountancy
2601 N. Third Street
Harrisburg, PA 17110
Phone: 717-783-1404
Fax: 717-705-5540
Web: www.dos.state.pa.us/account

Puerto Rico Board of Accountancy
Box 9023271
Old San Juan Station
San Juan, PR 00902-3271
Phone: 787-722-4816
Fax: 787-722-4818
Web: www.estado.gobierno.pr/contador.htm

Rhode Island Board of Accountancy
233 Richmond Street, Suite 236
Providence, RI 02903-4236
Phone: 401-222-3185
Fax: 401-222-6654
E-mail: boa@dbr.state.ri.us
Web: www.dbr.state.ri.us

South Carolina Board of Accountancy
110 Centerview Drive–Kingstree Building
P.O. Box 11329
Columbia, SC 29211
Phone: 803-896-4770
Fax: 803-896-4554
Web: www.llr.state.sc.us/POL/Accountancy/Default.htm

South Dakota Board of Accountancy
301 E. 14th Street, Suite 200
Sioux Falls, SD 57104
Phone: 605-367-5770
Fax: 605-367-5773
E-mail: sdbdacct.sdbd@midconetwork.com
Web: www.state.sd.us/dcr/accountancy

Tennessee State Board of Accountancy
500 James Robertson Parkway, 2nd Floor
Nashville, TN 37243-1141
Phone: 615-741-2550
Fax: 615-532-8800
E-mail: tnsba@mail.state.tn.us
Web: www.state.tn.us/commerce/boards/tnsba/index.html

Texas State Board of Public Accountancy
333 Guadalupe, Tower III, Suite 900
Austin, TX 78701-3900
Phone: 512-305-7800
Fax: 512-305-7854
Web: www.tsbpa.state.tx.us

Utah Board of Accountancy
P.O. Box 146741
Salt Lake City, UT 84114-6741
Phone: 801-530-6396
Fax: 801-530-6511
Web: www.dopl.utah.gov

Vermont Board of Public Accountancy
Office of Professional Regulation
26 Terrace Street, Drawer 09
Montpelier, VT 05609-1106
Phone: 802-828-2837
Fax: 802-828-2465
Web: www.vtprofessionals.org/opr1/accountants

Virgin Islands Board of Public Accountancy
Dept. of Licensing & Consumer Affairs
Office of Boards and Commissions
Golden Rock Shopping Center
Christiansted, St. Croix, VI 00820
Phone: 340-773-4305
Fax: 340-773-9850
Web: www.dlca.gov.vi

Virginia Board of Accountancy
3600 W. Broad Street, Suite 696
Richmond, VA 23230-4916
Phone: 804-367-8505
Fax: 804-367-2174
E-mail: boa@boa.state.va.us
Web: www.boa.state.va.us

Washington State Board of Accountancy
P.O. Box 9131
Olympia, WA 98507-9131
Phone: 360-753-2585
Fax: 360-664-9190
Web: www.cpaboard.wa.gov

West Virginia Board of Accountancy
122 Capitol Street, Suite 100
Charleston, WV 25301
Phone: 304-558-3557
Fax: 304-558-1325
E-mail: wvboa@mail.wvnet.edu
Web: www.state.wv.us/wvboa/

Wisconsin Accounting Examining Board
1400 E. Washington Avenue
P.O. Box 8935
Madison, WI 53708-8935
Phone: 608-266-5511
Fax: 608-267-3816
Web: www.drl.state.wi.us

Wyoming Board of Certified Public Accountants
2020 Carey Avenue
Cheyenne, WY 82002-0610
Phone: 307-777-7551
Fax: 307-777-3796
Web: cpaboard.state.wy.us

State Societies and Associations

Following is a listing of state societies and associations. These state societies and associations are useful resources. Most of them have online or printed classified pages to help you identify practices for sale or, possibly, to help you identify buyers searching for practices to acquire.

State EA Societies

The following information on state EA societies is current as of March 2005. For updates to this information, please visit the National Association of Enrolled Agents' Web site at www.naea.org.

Alabama Society of EAs
P.O. Box 242
Arab, AL 35016
Phone: 256-586-4111
Fax: 256-586-4138
Web: www.alsea.org

Alaska Society of EAs
P.O. Box 2163
Kodiak, AK 99615
Phone: 907-486-6225
Fax: 907-486-4129

Arizona Society of EAs
7360 E. 22nd Street, #109
Tucson, AZ 85710
Phone: 520-722-8363
Fax: 520-722-8398
Web: www.aztaxpros.org

Arkansas Society of EAs
15493 Riches Road
Fayetteville, AR 72704
Phone: 479-521-0310
Fax: 479-521-2269
Web: www.arksea.org

California Society of EAs
3200 Ramos Circle
Sacramento, CA 95827-2513
Phone: 916-366-6646
Fax: 916-366-6674
Web: www.csea.org

Colorado Society of EAs
6535 S. Dayton Street
Englewood, CO 80111
Phone: 303-708-8077
Fax: 303-708-8079
Web: www.taxpro.org

Connecticut Society of EAs
1111 E. Putnam Avenue
Riverside, CT 06878
Phone: 203-637-3887
Fax: 203-627-7965

Florida Society of EAs
P.O. Box 3877
Clearwater, FL 33767
Phone: 800-422-3732
Fax: 727-466-0830
Web: www.fseaonline.org

Georgia Association of EAs
424 Cove Drive
Marietta, GA 30067
Phone: 770-973-0764
Web: www.4gaea.org

Hawaii Society of EAs
P.O. Box 61397
Honolulu, HI 96839-1397
Phone: 808-589-2322
Fax: 808-589-2422

Illinois Society of EAs
1415 Matanuska Trail
McHenry, IL 60050
Phone: 815-385-6889
Fax: 815-363-1623

Indiana Society of EAs
202 E. Main Street
Danville, IN 46122
Phone: 317-745-6051
Fax: 317-745-1735
Web: www.indianaenrolledagents.com

Iowa Society of EAs
4415 Stone Avenue
Sioux City, IA 51106
Phone: 712-276-9240

Kentucky Society of EAs
8333 Alexandria Pike, Suite 204
Alexandria, KY 41101
Phone: 859-694-3000
Fax: 859-448-2762

Louisiana Society of EAs
2160 Park Drive
Slidell, LA 70458
Phone: 985-645-9031
Fax: 985-643-0710

Maryland/DC Society of EAs
550M Ritchie Highway, #145
Serverna Park, MD 21146
Phone: 410-544-4680
Fax: 410-544-1324

Massachusetts Society of EAs
100 Doyle Road
Holden, MA 01520
Phone: 508-853-9638
Fax: 508-852-0422

Michigan Society of EAs
1071 E. Nine Mile Road
Hazel Park, MI 48030
Phone: 248-547-99EA
Fax: 248-547-9934

Minnesota Society of EAs
P.O. Box 104
Clearwater, MN 55320-0104
Phone: 320-558-6800
Fax: 320-558-6019
Web: www.mnsea.org

Mississippi Society of EAs
P.O. Box 12304
Jackson, MS 39236-2304
Phone: 601-798-3116
Fax: 601-798-5650
Web: www.mssea.org

Missouri Society of EAs
1800 Liberty Park Boulevard, #6
Sedalia, MO 65301
Phone: 660-827-3212
Web: www.naea.org/mosea

Nevada Society of EAs
2585 S. Jones Boulevard, Suite 2D
Las Vegas, NV 89146-5604
Phone: 702-646-4646
Fax: 702-364-4697

New Jersey Society of EAs
11 New York Boulevard
Edison, NJ 08820-2423
Phone: 732-548-8023
Toll-free referral line: 877-652-6232
Fax: 732-548-8023
Web: www.njsea.org

New Mexico Society of EAs
3900 Paseo del Sol
Santa Fe, NM 87507
Phone: 505-988-9572
Fax: 505-988-9572

New York State Society of EAs
15 Reitz Parkway
Pittsford, NY 14534
Phone: 585-381-8585
Fax: 585-442-8252
Web: www.nyssea.org

North Carolina Society of EAs
4801 E. Independence Boulevard, Suite 903
Charlotte, NC 28212
Phone: 704-537-2067
Fax: 704-568-0956
Web: www.nc-sea.org

Northern New England Society of EAs
P.O. Box 331
Rye, NH 03870
Phone: 603-964-7177
Fax: 603-964-9030

Ohio State Society of EAs
5578 Worcester Drive
Columbus, OH 43232
Phone & fax: 614-861-3666
Web: www.ossea.org

Oklahoma Society of EAs
P.O. Box 337
Cordell, OK 73632
Phone: 405-832-3336
Fax: 405-832-3337

Oregon Society of EAs
1603 Oak Street
Eugene, OR 97401
Phone: 541-607-9200
Fax: 541-607-1770

Pennsylvania Society of EAs
677 West DeKalb Pike
King of Prussia, PA 19406
Phone: 610-337-2220
Fax: 610-265-7801

Rhode Island Society of EAs
1665 Hartford Avenue, Suite 3
Johnston, RI 02919
Phone: 401-274-8299
Fax: 401-273-6646

South Carolina Society of EAs
400 Stratford Drive
Summerville, SC 29485-8642
Phone: 843-871-1065
Fax: 843-871-1332

Tennessee Society of EAs
520 W. Richmond Shop Road
Lebanon, TN 37090
Phone: 615-444-6637
Web: www.tnsea.com

Utah Society of EAs
P.O. Box 26
Layton, UT 84041
Phone: 801-547-1152
Fax: 801-547-1170
Web: www.utsea.com

Texas Society of EAs
14350 Northbrook Drive, Suite 240
San Antonio, TX 78232
Phone: 210-402-6300
Fax: 210-402-2888
Web: www.txsea.org

Virginia Society of EAs
13208 Sherri Drive
Chester, VA 23831-4540
Phone: 804-748-4733
Toll-free: 800-344-8732
Fax: 804-748-2318
Web: www.vaeas.org

Washington State Society of EAs
222 E. Fourth Avenue, Suite A
Ellensburg, WA 98926
Phone: 509-925-6931
Toll-free: 800-613-2801
Fax: 509-962-5807
Web: www.taxea.org

Wisconsin Society of EAs
200 South Washington Street, #301
Green Bay, WI 54301
Phone: 920-432-6466
Fax: 920-432-5751

State CPA Societies and Associations

Alabama Society of CPAs
1103 South Perry Street
Montgomery, AL 36104
Phone: 334-834-7650
Toll-free instate: 800-227-1711
Fax: 334-834-7310
Web: www.ascpa.org

Alaska Society of CPAs
341 W. Tudor Road, #105
Anchorage, AK 99503
Phone: 907-562-4334
Toll-free instate: 800-478-4334
Fax: 907-562-4025
Web: www.akcpa.org

Arizona Society of CPAs
2120 N. Central Avenue, Suite 100
Phoenix, AZ 85004
Phone: 602-252-4144
Toll-free instate: 888-237-0700
Fax: 602-252-1511
Web: www.ascpa.com

Arkansas Society of CPAs
11300 Executive Center Drive
Little Rock, AR 72211-4352
Phone: 501-664-8739
Toll-free instate: 800-482-8739
Fax: 501-664-8320
Web: www.arcpa.org

California Society of CPAs
1235 Radio Road
Redwood City, CA 94065-1217
Phone: 800-922-5272
Web: www.calcpa.org

Colorado Society of CPAs
7979 E. Tufts Avenue, Suite 500
Denver, CO 80237-2845
Phone: 303-773-2877
Toll-free instate: 800-523-9082
Fax: 303-773-6344
Web: www.cocpa.org

Connecticut Society of CPAs
845 Brook Street, Building 2
Rocky Hill, CT 06067-3405
Phone: 860-258-4800
Toll-free instate: 800-232-2232
Fax: 860-258-4859
Web: www.cs-cpa.org

Delaware Society of CPAs
3512 Silverside Road
8 The Commons
Wilmington, DE 19810
Phone: 302-478-7442
Fax: 302-478-7412
Web: www.dscpa.org

Greater Washington Society of CPAs
1828 L Street NW, Suite 900
Washington, DC 20036
Phone: 202-204-8014
Fax: 202-204-8015
Web: www.gwscpa.org

Florida Institute of CPAs
325 W. College Avenue
Tallahassee, FL 32301
Phone: 850-224-2727
Toll-free instate: 800-342-3197
Fax: 850-222-8190
Web: www1.ficpa.org

Georgia Society of CPAs
3353 Peachtree Road NE, Suite 400
Atlanta, GA 30326-1026
Phone: 404-231-8676
Toll-free instate: 800-330-8889
Fax: 404-237-1291
Web: www.gscpa.org

Hawaii Society of CPAs
900 Fort Street Mall, Suite 850
Honolulu, HI 96813
Phone: 808-537-9475
Fax: 808-537-3520
Web: www.hscpa.org

Idaho Society of CPAs
250 Bobwhite Court, Suite 240
Boïse, ID 83706
Phone: 208-344-6261
Fax: 208-344-8984
Web: www.idcpa.org

Illinois CPA Society (Chicago Office)
550 W. Jackson, Suite 900
Chicago, IL 60661-5716
Phone: 312-993-0407
Toll-free instate: 800-993-0407
Fax: 312-993-9954
Web: www.icpas.org

Indiana CPA Society
8250 Woodfield Crossing Boulevard, #100
Indianapolis, IN 46240-4348
Phone: 317-726-5000
Fax: 317-726-5005
Web: http://incpas.org

Iowa Society of CPAs
950 Office Park Road, Suite 300
West Des Moines, IA 50265-2548
Phone: 515-223-8161
Toll-free instate: 800-659-6375
Fax: 515-223-7347
Web: www.iacpa.org

Kansas Society of CPAs
1080 S.W. Wanamaker Road, Suite 200
P.O. Box 4291
Topeka, KS 66604
Phone: 785-272-4366
Fax: 785-272-4468
Web: www.kscpa.org

Maine Society of CPAs
153 U.S. Route 1, Suite 8
Scarborough, ME 04074-9053
Phone: 207-883-6090
Toll-free instate: 800-660-2721
Fax: 207-883-6211
Web: http://www.mecpa.org

Kentucky Society of CPAs
1735 Alliant Avenue
Louisville, KY 40299
Phone: 502-266-5272
Toll-free: 800-292-1754
Fax: 502-261-9512
Web: www.kycpa.org

Society of Louisiana CPAs
2400 Veterans Memorial Boulevard, Suite 500
Kenner, LA 70062
Phone: 504-464-1040
Toll-free: 800-288-5272
Fax: 504-469-7930
Web: www.lcpa.org

Maryland Association of CPAs
Dulaney Center II
901 Dulaney Valley Road, Suite 710
Towson, MD 21204-2683
Phone: 410-296-6250
Toll-free: 800-782-2036
Fax: 410-296-8713
Web: www.macpa.org

Massachusetts Society of CPAs
105 Chauncy Street, 10th floor
Boston, MA 02111
Phone: 617-556.4000
Toll free: 800-392.6145
Fax: 617-556.4126
Web: www.mscpaonline.org

Michigan Association of CPAs
P.O. Box 5068
Troy, MI 48007-5068
Phone: 248-267-3700
Toll-free: 888-877-4CPE
Fax: 248-267-3737
Web: www.michcpa.org

Minnesota Society of CPAs
1650 W. 82nd Street, Suite 600
Bloomington, MN 55431
Phone: 952-831-2707
Toll-free: 800-331-4288
Fax: 952-831-7875
Web: www.mncpa.org

Mississippi Society of CPAs
Highland Village, Suite 246
Jackson, MS 39211
Phone: 601-366-3473
Toll-free instate: 800-772-1099
Fax: 601-981-6079
Web: www.ms-cpa.org

Missouri Society of CPAs
275 N. Lindbergh Boulevard, Suite 10
St. Louis, MO 63141-7809
Phone: 314-997-7966
Toll-free instate: 800-264-7966
Fax: 314-997-2592
Web: www.mocpa.org

Nebraska Society of CPAs
635 S. 14th Street, Suite 330
Lincoln, NE 68508
Phone: 402-476-8482
Toll-free: 800-642-6178
Fax: 402-476-8731
Web: www.nescpa.com

Nevada Society of CPAs (Reno Office)
5250 Neil Road, Suite 205
Reno, NV 89502
Phone: 775-826-6800
Toll-free: 800-554-8254
Fax: 775-826-7942
Web: www.nevadacpa.org

New Hampshire Society of CPAs
1750 Elm Street, Suite 403
Manchester, NH 03104
Phone: 603-622-1999
Fax: 603-626-0204
Web: www.nhscpa.org

New Jersey Society of CPAs
425 Eagle Rock Avenue
Roseland, NJ 07068-1723
Phone: 973-226-4494
Fax: 973-226-7425
Web: www.njscpa.org

New Mexico Society of CPAs
1650 University NE, Suite 450
Albuquerque, NM 87102
Phone: 505-246-1699
Toll-free: 800-926-2522
Fax: 505-246-1686
Web: www.nmscpa.org

New York State Society of CPAs
3 Park Avenue, 18th Floor
New York, NY 10016-5991
Phone: 212-719-8300
Toll-free: 800-NYSSCPA
Fax: 212-719-3364
Web: www.nysscpa.org

North Carolina Association of CPAs
3100 Gateway Centre Boulevard
Morrisville, NC 27560-9241
Phone: 919-469-1040
Toll-free: 800-722-2836
Fax: 919-469-3959
Web: www.ncacpa.org

North Dakota CPA Society
2701 S. Columbia Road
Grand Forks, ND 58201
Phone: 701-775-7100
Toll-free: 877-637-2727
Fax: 701-775-7430
Web: www.ndscpa.org

Ohio State Society of CPAs
535 Metro Place South
Dublin, OH 43017
Phone: 614-764-2727
Toll-free: 800-686-2727
Fax: 614-764-5880
Web: www.ohioscpa.com

Oklahoma Society of CPAs
1900 N.W. Expressway, Suite 910
Oklahoma City, OK 73118-1898
Phone: 405-841-3800
Toll-free: 800-522-8261
Fax: 405-841-3801
Web: www.oscpa.com

Oregon Society of CPAs
10206 S.W. Laurel Street
Beaverton, OR 97005-3209
Phone: 503-641-7200
Toll-free: 800-255-1470
Fax: 503-626-2942
Web: www.orcpa.org

Pennsylvania Institute of CPAs
1650 Arch Street, 17th Floor
Philadelphia, PA 19103
Phone: 215-496-9272
Toll-free instate: 888-CPA-2001
Fax: 215-496-9212
Web: www.picpa.org

Rhode Island Society of CPAs
45 Royal Little Drive
Providence, RI 02904
Phone: 401-331-5720
Fax: 401-454-5780
Web: www.riscpa.org

South Carolina Association of CPAs
570 Chris Drive
West Columbia, SC 29169
Phone: 803-791-4181
Toll-free instate: 888-557-4814
Fax: 803-791-4196
Web: www.scacpa.org

South Dakota CPA Society
1000 N. West Avenue, #100
P.O. Box 1798
Sioux Falls, SD 57101-1798
Phone: 605-334-3848
Fax: 605-334-8595
Web: www.sdcpa.org

Vermont Society of CPAs
100 State Street, Suite 500
Montpelier, VT 05602
Phone: 802 229-4939
Fax: 802 223-0360
Web: www.vtcpa.org

Tennessee Society of CPAs
201 Powell Place
Brentwood, TN 37027
Phone: 615-377-3825
Toll-free: 800-762-0272
Fax: 615-377-3904
Web: www.tscpa.com

Texas Society of CPAs
14860 Montfort Drive, Suite 150
Dallas, TX 75254-6705
Phone: 972-687-8500
Toll-free: 800-428-0272
Fax: 972-687-8696
Web: www.tscpa.org

Utah Society of CPAs
9449 Union Square, #200
Sandy, UT 84070
Phone: 801-571-2870
Fax: 801-571-2891
Web: www.utsea.com

Virginia Society of CPAs
4309 Cox Road
Glen Allen, VA 23060
Phone: 804-270-5344
Toll-free: 800-733-8272
Fax: 804-273-1741
Web: www.vscpa.com

Washington Society of CPAs
902 140th Avenue NE
Bellevue, WA 98005-3480
Phone: 425-644-4800
Toll-free instate: 800-272-8273
Fax: 425-562-8853
Web: www.wscpa.org

West Virginia Society of CPA's
900 Lee Street E, Suite 1201
Charleston, WV 25301
Phone: 304-342-5461
Fax: 304-344-4636
Web: www.wvscpa.org

Wisconsin Institute of CPAs
235 N. Executive Drive, Suite 200
Brookfield, WI 53005
Phone: 262-785-0445
Toll-free: 800-772-6939
Fax: 262-785-0838
Web: www.wicpa.org

Wyoming Society of CPAs
1603 Capitol Avenue, Suite 413
Cheyenne, WY 82001
Phone: 307-634-7039
Fax: 307-634-5110
Web: www.wyocpa.org

General Business Acquisition Terms

Acceleration Clause
A clause used in a note and/or security agreement, which gives the lender the right to demand payment in full if a certain event occurs such as default or if the ownership of the business changes without the lender's consent. Sometimes referred to as a "due on sale" clause.

Acceptance
The act of accepting an offer which results in a binding contract.

Acknowledgment
A declaration, by a person qualified by law to administer oaths, that the person signing a document or a deed is the person he or she claims to be.

Addendum
A written instrument that adds something to a written contract.

Agency

The legal relationship between a principal and his agent arising from a contract in which the principal engages the agent to perform certain acts on the principal's behalf.

Agency Listing

A written instrument giving the agent the right to sell property for a specified time. However, the owner may sell the property himself or herself to a buyer who was not introduced to the business by the agent without the payment of a commission to the agent.

Agency Disclosure

A written explanation to be signed by a prospective buyer or seller, explaining to the client the role that the broker plays in the transaction. The purpose of disclosure is to explain whether the broker represents the buyer or seller or is a dual agent (representing both) or a subagent (an agent of the seller's broker). This allows the customer to understand to which party the broker owes loyalty.

Agent

One acting under authority of a principal to do the principal's business. The agent must use his or her best efforts and keep the principal fully informed of all material facts.

Allocation

A breakdown of the purchase price usually required when a business is sold. For example, the allocation might contain a breakdown of the inventories, fixtures and equipment, leasehold improvements, goodwill, and any other purchased assets. Generally, value is placed on each component of the allocation, and the buyer and seller agree on this breakdown. The IRS requires that such an allocation be a part of the buyer's and seller's tax returns when a sale takes place. Form 8594, the "asset acquisition statement," must be filed with the buyer's and seller's tax returns for the year in which an *applicable asset acquisition* takes place.

Amendment
A written instrument that changes something previously agreed to. (This is different from an addendum.)

Amortization
1. A reduction in a debt obligation by periodic payments covering interest, and part of the principal. 2. The writing off or expensing of the cost of intangible assets over a period of time, usually in years. Amortization of intangible assets versus depreciation of tangible assets. Intangible assets purchased, such as goodwill and covenants-not-to-compete, can be written off over fifteen years.

Appreciation
A gain in value due to any cause. Real estate is an asset that often appreciates in value over time.

Arbitration
The submission of a disputed matter for resolution outside the normal judicial system. It is often speedier and less costly than courtroom procedures. An arbitration award can be enforced legally in court. If one or more parties cannot agree on a single arbitrator, they can select arbitrators under the rules of the American Arbitration Association. Arbitration clauses are often inserted into contracts as the forum to settle disputes arising out of the contract.

Asking Price
The total amount for which a business or an ownership interest is offered for sale.

Asset Sale
A sale of a business in which the buyer acquires only specific assets (and possibly assumes some liabilities). Unlike a stock sale, the buyer obtains the assets usually free and clear of any liabilities of the seller. The buyer also gets the advantage of a "step-up" in

basis on the assets purchased based on their allocated fair market values.

Attorney-In-Fact
One who is appointed, in writing, to perform a specific act for and in place of another; e.g., signing documents for someone in their absence.

Base Rent
The minimum rent in a lease, which sometimes contains a percentage or provisions for additional rent.

Bill of Sale
A written agreement by which one person assigns or transfers his or her rights to or interest in goods and personal property to another.

Blue-Sky
An expression sometimes used to label the intangible assets (e.g., goodwill) in the purchase of a business enterprise.

Bond
A pledge to pay a sum of money in the event of failure to fulfill obligations; e.g., inflicting damage or mishandling funds. Usually written by a company for a fee. Also known as a surety bond.

Breach of Contract
Failure of a party to a contract to perform any or all of his or her obligations under the contract.

Broker
One who acts as an agent for another (his or her principal) when negotiating with third parties on behalf of the principal. This arrangement falls under "agency" law applicable in the state in which the principal-agent arrangements arises.

Bulk Sale

A transfer in bulk of all or substantially all of the inventory and fixtures of a business which is not in the ordinary course of business.

Bulk Sales Act

Laws enacted by the states to protect creditors against secret sales of all or substantially all of a business's goods. It requires certain notices prior to the sale and sets forth ways of voiding the sale (see Uniform Commercial Code).

Business Broker

A business broker is an intermediary dedicated to serving clients and customers who desire to sell or acquire businesses. A business broker is committed to providing professional services in a knowledgeable, ethical, and timely fashion. Typically, business brokers provide information and business advice to sellers and buyers, maintain communications between the parties, and coordinate the negotiations and closing processes to complete desired transactions.

Business Personal Property

Business personal property is defined as all tangible and intangible personal property and rights in personal property owned by a seller and used in the business, including furniture; trade fixtures and equipment; tools used in business; telephone numbers and listings, if transferable; customer lists; trade names; business records; supplies; leases; advance lease deposits; customer deposits; signs; all other personal property used in business; and if transferable, all permits, special licenses, and franchises, except those assets disposed of in the ordinary course of business or as permitted by this offer.

Business Trade Name

Company name by which a certain business is known. Also know as the DBA, "doing business as," or T/A, "trading as."

Buyer Agreement
Document used by business intermediaries to protect the seller's confidentiality and the broker's fee.

Cancellation Clause
A clause in a lease or other contract stating the condition(s) under which the contract can be canceled or terminated by any of the parties. It may provide for simple notice or possible payment of money to cancel the contract.

Cashier's Check
A check drawn on the bank's own funds. It is often used to close a sale because there is generally no waiting for the check to clear.

Caveat Emptor
"Let the buyer beware" indicates the responsibility of the purchaser to protect oneself with reasonable caution.

Certified Check
A personal check guaranteed by the bank. The bank holds the necessary funds and will not accept any withdrawals against the certified amount. The bank also will not usually honor a stop payment on a certified check.

Chattel (U.C.C.) Search
A chattel is an article of personal property, and it includes both animate and inanimate property. U.C.C. stands for the Uniform Commercial Code, which governs the granting of security agreements. A chattel search is a review of the appropriate county and secretary of state records in regard to any liens against chattels, tax liens, and judgments.

Chattel Mortgage
A mortgage on personal property (not real estate). A mortgage on equipment would be a chattel mortgage.

Client
An entity with which a business broker has a fiduciary relationship.

Co-brokerage
An agreement between two or more business brokers for sharing services, responsibility, and compensation on behalf of a client.

Co-business Broker
A business broker who shares services, responsibility, and compensation on behalf of a client.

Confidentiality Agreement
A pact that forbids buyers, sellers, and their agents in a given business deal from disclosing information about the transaction to others.

Consideration
Something of value that induces a person to enter into a contract. The promise to do something must be in exchange for some act or thing of value which is the consideration. This is a necessary element in a contract.

Contract
A voluntary and lawful agreement between two or more parties to do, or not to do, something. Elements of an enforceable contract include: (a) an offer to be bound to do or refrain from doing something, which has been accepted; (b) sufficient consideration; (c) a valid subject matter; (d) legal capacity of the parties; and (e) for those contracts to which the statute of fraud applies, its requirements must be met.

Conveyance
A transfer of title.

Cooperating Business Brokers
Business brokers who share their knowledge, expertise, and skills for the benefit of the business brokerage profession, clients, customers, and the public good.

Corporation
An entity created by or under the authority of the laws of a state, composed of individuals united under a common name, and which for certain legal purposes is considered a natural person. Characteristics of a corporation include: (a) continuity of life, (b) centralization of management, (c) limited liability, and (d) free transferability of interest.

Closing
When all the details of the business sale are completed and the money is distributed to the seller, seller's agents, creditors, and others.

Closing Documents
The legal documents that are part of a business closing. They might include: a definitive purchase contract, promissory notes, mortgage, security agreements, financing statements, subordination agreements, bill of sale, covenant-not-to-compete, consulting agreements, employment agreements, leases, assignments, escrow agreement, releases, tax clearances, director and shareholder consents, legal opinions, environmental opinions, fairness opinions, and an asset acquisition statement.

Closing Statement
A statement that contains the financial settlements between the buyer and seller and the cost each must pay. This information may be on one statement, or the buyer and seller may each receive separate statements.

Conditional Sales Contract

This is different from a chattel mortgage. Title to the goods, fixtures and equipment, or the business itself remains with the seller and is not transferred to the buyer, until the terms of the contract have been met. This generally means when all the payments have been made.

Contingency

A clause in an agreement, contract, escrow, etc. that is only binding upon the occurrence of a stated event. For example, the sale of the business is contingent upon the buyer obtaining financing.

Covenant

A promise in an agreement or contract agreeing to performance or nonperformance of certain acts, or requiring or preventing certain acts or uses.

Covenant-Not-To-Compete

An agreement made part of a purchase contract, in which the seller promises not to enter into a similar or competing business, for a specified period of time, within a designated area.

Creditor

A person to whom a debt is owed by another person who is called the debtor.

Customer

An entity to a transaction who receive services and benefits, but has no fiduciary relationship with the business broker.

DBA

"Doing business as" is an identification of the trade name of the business, which may differ from the legal corporate name.

Demand Note
A promissory note that has no set time period for repayment and can be called due by the holder at any time.

Directors
Those who are elected by the stockholders to manage the affairs of a corporation. Shareholders elect directors; directors elect officers; officers manage the day-to-day affairs of a corporation.

Disclaimer
A statement that attempts to limit liability in the event information is inaccurate.

Discretionary Earnings
The earnings of a business enterprise prior to the following items:

- Income taxes

- Nonoperating income and expenses

- Nonrecurring income and expenses

- Depreciation and amortization

- Interest expense or income

- Owner's total compensation for those services which could be provided by a sole owner/manager

Due Diligence
Investigation of the target company in an acquisition on behalf of or by the potential acquirer, in order to determine whether the target company is worth buying and what its true market value is. The target company permits the acquirer to evaluate the target's assets, profits, market share positions, technology, customer franchise, patents and brand rights, and contracts. Due diligence is often performed on the acquirer as well as the target.

Duress
Unlawful constraint exercised upon a person whereby he or she is forced to do some act against his or her will.

Earnest Money
A sum of money given to bind an agreement or an offer.

Economic Life
The "profitable" life of fixtures and equipment or any improvement; this life could be greater or less than the depreciable life for income tax purposes.

Escalation Clause
A clause, generally in a lease, that provides for an increase in the rent at a specified time.

Escrow
A deed, a bond, money, or other piece of property delivered to a third person to be delivered by him or her to the grantee only upon the fulfillment of a condition.

Exclusive Right to Sell Listing
When a business owner gives only one broker or agent the authority to sell his or her business. The broker or agent receives commission no matter who sells the business—even if the seller finds the buyer during the listing period.

Execute
To complete, to make, to perform, to do, to follow through; to execute a contract; to make a contract: especially signing, sealing, and delivery.

Fictitious Name
The name of a business that is different from the legal entity. In most areas, this name needs to be filed with a state, county, or local government agency to be legally effective. Also known as "DBA."

Fiduciary
Acting in a relationship or position of trust, usually regarding financial matters or transactions.

Financing Statement
A recorded document filed generally in the secretary of state's office and shows that there is a lien against the fixtures and equipment (personal property) of the business.

Finder's Fee
An amount paid to another party for locating and referring a client or customer.

Fixture
An item of property which is physically attached to or so closely associated with land or a building as to be treated as part of the real estate including, without limitation, physically attached items not easily removable without damage to the property, items specifically adapted to the property, and items customarily treated as fixtures.

Franchise
The right or license granted to an individual or group (franchisee) to market a company's (franchisor's) goods or services in a particular geographic territory.

Indemnification
A promise by one party to another to restore a loss by payment of money, replacement, or repair. They are used typically to cover the result of a warranty or representation that is or was not true.

Graduated Lease
A lease that calls for periodic increases in the rent.

Hard Assets (also referred to as "tangible assets")
Those assets which are material or physical (e.g., inventory, equipment, tools, vehicles, real estate, leasehold improvements).

Indemnity
Payment that compensates for an incurred loss or damage.

Instrument
A written legal document created to affect the rights of the parties.

Intangible Asset
That which has no physical existence but represents value, such as goodwill, going concern value, business trade name (see blue-sky).

Irrevocable
Incapable of being recalled or canceled; unchangeable.

Joint Tenancy
Same as tenancy in common, but if one party dies, his or her title passes to the surviving joint tenant(s), and not to the heirs of the decedent.

Joint Venture
A business arrangement between two or more persons. Similar to a partnership except that it exists to undertake a single project.

Lease
A written legal document in which possession of a property is given by the owner (lessor) to second party (lessee) for a specified time and for a specified rent, and setting forth the conditions upon which the lessee may use and/or occupy the property.

Lease with Option to Purchase
A lease in which the lessee has the right to purchase the property for a stipulated price at or within a stipulated time.

Leasehold
A property held under tenure of lease; a property consisting of the right of use and occupancy by virtue of a lease agreement; the lessee's (tenant's) interest in a lease.

Leasehold Improvements
Any article or fixture that is attached to land or buildings.

Legal Description
The legal identification of real property.

Lessee
A tenant; one who has a right to occupy the premises by virtue of a lease.

Lessor
A landlord; one who grants a right to the lessee to occupy the premises by virtue of a lease.

Letter of Intent
A document agreement between a buyer and a seller used in connection with the acquisition of a company. The letter of intent describes the basic terms and conditions of the transaction between the buyer and the seller, including price, due diligence periods, exclusivity or no-shops, and the basic conditions to closing the deal. Customarily presented before a definitive purchase agreement is entered into, the letter of intent provides a road map for the parties involved in the transaction.

Lien
A claim or charge upon real or personal property for the satisfaction of some debt or duty which can arise either by agreement or by operation of law.

Limited Partnership
A partnership composed of some partners whose contributions and liabilities are limited. A limited partnership requires at least one general partner and one limited partner. The general partner(s) are responsible for the management and liability for its debts. A limited partner has no right in management, and his or her liability is limited to amount of investment.

Listing
A written engagement (contract) between a principal and an agent authorizing the agent to perform services for the principal involving the principal's property (business). Generally, the services provided by the agent involve the proposed sale of the principal's property or business. Also, the property or business listed by the agent is called a listing.

Mediation
A voluntary non-binding settlement arranged by a third party. Not normally used in a purchase agreement.

Merger
Any combination that forms one company from two or more previously existing companies.

Misrepresentation
A statement contrary to fact. If the statement or action is made with intent to deceive, it may be deemed to be fraudulent.

Negligence
Failure to act like a reasonably prudent person to protect the interest or safety of others.

Negotiable
Capable of being negotiated; assignable or transferable in the ordinary course of business.

Net-Net-Net Lease (triple net lease)
A lease in which the tenant (lessee) pays a pro-rata share of normal property expenses such as real estate taxes, insurance, maintenance, etc., thereby assuring the landlord (lessor) of a fixed income.

Net Listing
A price which must be expressly agreed upon, below which the owner (principal) will not sell the property and at which price the agent will not receive a commission; the agent receives the excess over and above the net listing as his or her commission. This type of commission is unlawful in some states.

Nonoperating\Noncontributing Asset
An asset unnecessary to the operation of a business enterprise and the generation of its revenues.

Offset (set-off)
A deduction by one against a claim of another; e.g., unknown claims against the assets purchased by a buyer may be "offset" against the obligation the buyer owes to the seller (seller financing).

Open Listing
A listing which is nonexclusive; may be given to any number of agencies without obligation to compensate any of them except the one that first secures a buyer ready, willing, and able to meet the terms of the listing, or that secures the acceptance by the seller of a satisfactory offer.

Option
A written agreement granting to a party the exclusive right, during a stated period of time, to buy or obtain control of property or assets on specified terms, but without any obligation of such party actually to exercise such option.

Owner
A generic term used in business brokerage to represent the proprietor, general partner, or controlling shareholder (singular or plural as appropriate) of a business enterprise.

Owner's Salary
The salary or wages paid to the owner, including related payroll burden. Not to be confused with owner's discretionary income.

Owner's Total Compensation
Total of an owner's salary and perquisites, after the compensation of all other owners has been adjusted to market value.

Partnership
A business relationship between two or more persons who join together to contribute to the capital and/or operations of an enterprise, and share the profits and losses (also, see limited partnership). Partnerships must lack two or more of the four corporate characteristics (see corporations) to be taxed as such.

Personal Property
Any property which is not real property; that which is not permanently affixed to the land.

Perquisites
Expenses incurred at the discretion of the owner which are unnecessary to the continued operation of the business.

Points
In the language of the loan business, a point is one percent of the amount of the loan.

Power of Attorney
An instrument authorizing a person to act as the agent of the person granting it. A general power of attorney authorizes the agent to act generally on behalf of his or her principal; a special power of attorney limits the agent to a specific or particular act.

Principal
The employer of an agent. Also, a sum of money owed excluding any accrued interest.

Promissory Note
A signed, written instrument which acknowledges a debt, with the promise to pay the debt on specified terms (i.e., payment amount, payment date(s), interest rate).

Procuring Cause
A legal term that means the cause resulting in accomplishing a goal. Used in real estate (or business brokerage) to determine whether a broker is entitled to a commission.

Proration
The division of money obligations according to some formula. In a business closing, a seller may have paid for certain benefits into the future which are assumed by the buyer. The cost of these benefits are "prorated" between the seller and the buyer as part of the closing statement (e.g., prepaid rent, prepaid advertising, security deposits).

Purchase Agreement
The agreement setting out the terms for the purchase of a business. A purchase agreement is the "road map" followed by the buyer and the seller in a business transaction. It includes items such as a description of what is being purchased, the down payment and repayment terms, buyer and seller representations, warranties, and indemnifications, and so on.

Referring Business Broker
A business broker who provides introductory information which leads to a client relationship.

Release
The relinquishment of some right or benefit by a person or entity who already has some interest or right therein.

Representation

A statement or condition made that something is true or accurate.

Small Business Administration (SBA) Lender Status

- **Certified Lender Program (CLP).** This process is for the more sophisticated and experienced lenders who have graduated beyond General Program (GP) status. Typically, the lender submits a complete package to the SBA and, as a CLP lender, is guaranteed a three-day turnaround from the SBA.

- **General Program (GP).** This is the lowest rating and is given to lenders that know little about the SBA process. These lenders must submit each loan application to the SBA for additional underwriting and ultimate approval. This process can take up to two weeks with multiple requests for additional information.

- **Preferred Lender Program (PLP).** This is the top designation and enables the respective lenders to approve their own loans with no additional underwriting by the SBA. Typically, this designation means that the lender has sufficient experience and track history to adhere to SBA standards and make quality loans.

S Corporation

A small business corporation which is treated differently than a C corporation for income tax purposes. Normally, it can be used by a corporation with seventy-five or fewer domestic shareholders when the corporation has only one class of stock. Individuals, another S corporation, estates, certain trusts, certain financial institutions, and tax-exempt organizations may own shares in an S corporation. An S corporation may own 100 percent of a C corporation. If all the statutory requirements are met, the shareholders can elect to have most of the corporation's income and deductions flow through to the shareholders in a manner similar to the taxation of a partnership.

Security Agreement
The agreement given by a debtor to a creditor giving the creditor a resource to look to in case the debtor fails to pay the principal obligation.

Simple Interest
The interest on principal only as compared to compound interest, which is interest on both principal and accumulated interest.

Sole Proprietorship
A business owned by one person or married persons. The owner is personally liable for the debts of the business. The business is not incorporated.

Statute of Frauds
State law which provides that certain contracts must be in writing in order to be enforceable by law; e.g., the sale of real property, a lease of real property for more than one year, broker's authorization to act as an agent on behalf of his or her principal.

Stipulation
To make a special demand for something as a condition of an agreement.

Stock Sale
The buyer purchases the stock in a corporation so the corporation is acquired in whole and the buyer obtains all assets and liabilities. Buyer gets no step up in basis in the underlying assets in the corporation (unless a not often used tax election is made).

Synergy
The post-acquisition performance, in which the profitability of the continued entity is greater than the sum of the profitability of the individual entities before the acquisition.

Sublease
A lease where the lessee can be the lessor, in effect, on a subsequent lease. The owner of the property often must approve in writing the tenant's right to sublease to a new tenant. This is different from a "master lease" where the lessee has greater control over subletting the property.

Subordination
The act of making an encumbrance secondary or junior to another lien.

Tenancy in Common
Two or more persons holding an undivided interest in the same property. Each tenant can dispose of his or her undivided interest by deed or by will; upon death, the interest descends to the heirs (see joint tenancy).

Title
Evidence that the person or entity claiming to be the owner of the property is in fact the lawful owner thereof; an instrument evidencing such ownership.

Title Insurance
Insures the interest of the buyer or mortgagee in real estate.

Transaction Value
The total of all consideration passed at any time between the buyer and seller for an ownership interest in a business enterprise and may include, but not limited to, all remuneration for tangible and intangible assets such as furniture, equipment, supplies, inventory, working capital, noncompetition agreements, employment and/or consultation agreements, licenses, customer lists, franchise fees, assumed liabilities, stock options, stock or stock redemptions, real estate, leases, royalties, earn-outs, and future considerations.

Uniform Commercial Code (U.C.C.)
State laws which regulate the transfer of personal property. Article nine of the U.C.C. deals with transactions which are intended to create a security interest in personal property.

Valid
Legally binding.

Void
To have no force or effect; that which is unenforceable.

Waive
To relinquish or abandon; to forego a right to enforce or require anything.

Warrant or Warranty
To legally assure or a legal or binding promise.

Without Recourse
The lender can only look to the security for the debt and cannot go after the buyer personally in the case of default. Often bank loans to closely held businesses require "personal guarantees" of the business owner(s).

INDEX

5 Cs of Credit 78, 82–83

Acquiring a firm 7–30
  acquisition model 57
  buyer motivations 49–51, 88, 109
  buying process 16–27
  determining size 16–17, 88
  existing firm vs. start-up 9–10,
    11
  legal advice 25
  pre-offer financial review 20–21,
    92–93
  questions on buying 7–8
  stock vs. asset sale 21
  tips for buyers 30
  types of buyers 8
American Express 2
Analysis paralysis 22, 111

Business sales memorandum 18,
    89, 91
  creating 42–43
Buyer motivations 49–51, 88, 109
Buying process 16–27

Capitalization rate 42
Cash revenue
  reporting 35

Client loss 74
  and client retention clauses 102
  planning for 103–5
Collateral 79, 83
Common mistakes
  being a lone ranger 111–15
  breaching confidentiality 105–7
  conducting insufficient due
    diligence 110–11
  focusing on one buyer 109
  not planning for client loss 103–5
  selling for too little 97–100
  selling to employee or partner
    107–8
  selling to wrong buyer 101
  settling on unsatisfactory terms
    101–3
  waiting too long to sell 109–10
  wasting time on unqualified
    buyers 100
Confidentiality agreement 19, 28,
    44, 91, 105
  sample of 129
Confidentiality breaches 43, 105–7
Counteroffer 22, 46, 93
CPA industry
  average size of firms 32
  changes in 2–3

Deal structures 37–42, 74–75
    Capitalization-of-Earnings
        Method 37
    Discounted-Future-Earnings
        Method 37
    earn-outs 37–39, 74, 102
    earnings capitalization 42
    excess earnings 42
    fixed price 39–40, 74
    multiple of annual gross billings
        40–41, 75
    net income multiples 41–42
Deals
    why they fall apart 27
Down payment 72, 93
Due diligence 22–24, 46, 77, 94,
    103
    checklist 111, 131–36
    in mergers 61
    insufficient 110–11

Extended Reporting Period
    Coverage 69

Fair market value
    determining 20
Financing 20, 71–84
    and due diligence 23
    by seller 72, 75, 76
    considerations 76
    elements of loan application
        package 80–82
    factors in loan approval 82–83
    methods 72–75
    questions on 71–72
    steps 77–78
    time it takes to secure a loan 83

Internet resources 121–22

Lending sources
    evaluating 78–80
Letter announcing sale to clients
    126
Letter introducing buyer to clients
    127
Letter of intent 21, 25, 93, 124
Life cycle of a sale 85–96

Marketing the sale of your practice
    43, 89, 109, 113
Mergers 57–70
    checklist 67–69
    finding a merger candidate 61
    good reasons to merge 59–60
    model 58
    negotiation steps 64–65
    pitfalls 65–66
    planning 61–63
    reasons to avoid 60–61
    why true mergers are so rare
        57–59

Negotiations 22, 46, 93

Offshore outsourcing 3
Owner perks 35

Partner or ownership agreement 65
Practice continuation agreement 4
Pre-offer financial review 20–21,
    45, 92–93
Purchase agreement 24–25,
    47–48, 77, 94
    elements of 24–25, 47–48

Sales plan
    preparing 34–35
Sales process 33–49
Seller motivations 32–33, 87

Selling a practice 31–55
  buyer's criteria 35
  for too little 97–100
  pre-offer financial review 45, 92–93
  questions on selling 31–32
  sales process 33–49
  seller motivations 32–33, 87
  setting a price 35–42, 97–100
  sizing up your practice 33–34, 87
  structures for valuing a business 37–42
  timing 51–52, 109–10, 118
  tips for sellers 55
Specialty brokers 17, 33, 87
  advantages to using 27–28, 52–53, 98
  selecting 113–15
  why use 27–28, 52–53

State boards of accountancy 137–48
State CPA societies and associations 156–65
State EA societies 149–55
Succession planning
  lack of 4

Terms and contingencies
  structuring 101–3
Transition 26, 49, 61–63, 96
  and retaining client base 74
  milestones 95–96

JOHN R. EZELL, CPA, is the president of ProHorizons—a brokerage and consulting firm specializing in the sale of accounting and tax practices. He has advised hundreds of clients in the sales, acquisitions, and mergers of accounting and tax firms since 1995.

Before founding and successfully selling his own CPA practice in the Washington, DC area, John worked with other firms including BDO Seidman, an international accounting and consulting firm.

John is a Certified Public Accountant licensed in California and a licensed California Real Estate Broker. He holds a BS in Accounting from George Mason University in Fairfax, Virginia. Prior to attending college, John served in the United States Marine Corps and was an Embassy Guard in Moscow and Berlin.

John and his wife, Jennifer, have four children. In his free time, he coaches youth baseball and soccer, and serves his community in a variety of volunteer leadership positions.

John can be reached at 800-729-3242 or john@prohorizons.com.

KEN BERRY is an independent marketing and business development consultant. He has worked closely with John Ezell and ProHorizons since June 2002. During that time, he has assisted in defining, developing, and refining ProHorizons' internal processes, its role in the accounting practice sales industry, and its level of service to and communication with its existing and potential clients.

Prior to his move into consulting, Ken spent nine years working in marketing and sales at Crisp Learning, a leading publisher of corporate training and personal improvement books, videos, and computer-based training programs.

Ken holds a BS in History from Willamette University in Salem, Oregon, and currently resides in the Silicon Valley.

In his free time, he plays soccer and hockey, skis, and coaches youth soccer.

Ken can be reached at 408-307-7343 or kberry@conexyn.com.